WE WERE KINGS

A DEEP DIVE INSIDE THE LIVES OF
PROFESSIONAL BEACH VOLLEYBALL PLAYERS

TRAVIS MEWHIRTER

CONTENTS

To my brothers, Cody and Tyler. No matter how many beaches I go to, my favorite place in the world is wherever y'all are. Wherever y'all are is home.

FORWARD

by Tri Bourne

feel very fortunate to be able to say that I've been a professional beach volleyball player since 2011. My first memory of playing beach volleyball is on the "baby court" at Outrigger (Canoe Club) in Waikiki, Hawaii. This is where I grew up. The ocean and the beach were my playground/daycare. I am almost positive that I spent more time at the club than I did at home (not including sleeping). Sometimes there were waves and sometimes there weren't, but the courts were always available. If they weren't it was because some of the other kids, who happened to be some of my best friends and now colleagues on tour, had already gotten the games started. When I wasn't at Outrigger or at a sporting event with my family, I was fascinated by watching pro sports on TV. And since we don't have pro sports in Hawaii, (besides the Pro Bowl, which I was at every year with my book of football cards to get autographed), actually playing sports for a living really did seem like just a dream. Although, I did grow up watching both of my parents compete in endurance sports both in the ocean and on land as amateur athletes and I would watch them push their bodies and minds to the limit like they were professionals, purely for the joy of competing. So I looked up to amateur athletes, but still I always dreamt of playing at the highest level. I guess in hindsight, being a professional beach volleyball player is exactly what I was raised to do.

Playing sports where the land meets the sea is where I've always found my happiness, but it wasn't enough to know that I could ball with the best on my island. So, I've looked to the mainland U.S. and overseas to compete with and against the best beach volleyball players that the world has to offer. My dream was to become an elite world class professional athlete. And beach volleyball has been the vehicle for me to chase that dream and see how far I can take it.

Being among the world's best athletes is what excites me. Each step of the process energizes me. The challenges motivate me. The harder the situation that I overcome the more confidence I gain. When I get to step out on stadium court it's like athlete heaven, knowing I've earned my spot and it's my time to do me. More pressure? More challenges? More Doubt? Yes, please! I love that shit!!

I've been asked, why do I continue to play beach volleyball when it's so hard to make a good living? Is it hard to make a good living? Because a good living is exactly what I have had and I just work hard to keep it. My "job" is to go to the beach and attempt to be a better athlete every day, to do exactly what I've done for years before making a penny. That's the definition of a good living, specifically for Tri Bourne. I play beach volleyball because I can. I can make a good living, I can make a ton of money, I can beat the struggles and I can continue to chase my dream of being one of the best athletes in the world. Plus, the real beauty in it all is the fact that it's hard. It's hard because our sport has grown to the point where only the elite will succeed. Those who hold that top spot get paid to train, to travel, to wear a brand's logo and often get paid just to show up. And they can have it all taken away in a second if they let up or if someone decides to take it from them. That competition in itself leads me to believe that beach volleyball as a sport and as a business is a success.

Beach volleyball has got to be the fastest growing sport in the world. As I'm writing this, my fellow Americans are playing in the world championships in Vienna, Austria. Thirty thousand people are on site to watch the final in the center court that 'only' holds 10,000 fans. That's about the same center court capacity as the Australian open (10,500), U.S. Open (10,200) and the French Open (10,056) in tennis. That being said, beach volleyball both domestically and on the international stage is more popular among fans and has more talent among the players right now than ever before.

Some of the old timers might say they disagree with me on that. In fact, I continue to hear about how we [today's players] need to do things more like they did back in the "heydey" and that's why we don't have that same great success on our domestic tour today. I've heard things like "this generation is boring to watch" because we don't play on an emotional rollercoaster or talk trash as much as they used to. "The players should be more fiery, more emotional, more entertaining and party harder like they used to." I've even heard an older player say that "Phil Dalhausser wouldn't be as dominant if he had to play back in the day on the big court." What a joke!

I have no intention of doing things like they used to. Rather I look to acknowledge and learn from what those before us have accomplished by setting the bar for our sport and continuing to raise it. I don't care that it used to be a lifestyle sport or that it still is for a few individuals. Sorry I'm not sorry about not carrying on that tradition; I'm not here for the parties.

I and at least the majority of the top 20 players in the USA are working every day to become more elite. That means sacrificing a lot of things that players used to get away with when our sport was just starting out and building on what the athletes have done through the 90s and early 2000s. Like the youngest sibling in a family, we as the new generation of athletes have the advantage of learning from what they did right or wrong and using it to better our lives and our sport. Truth is, we see ourselves as world class athletes who are looking for every advantage to be better while sacrificing and eliminating any distractions and that's why our sport continues to grow. Like my trainer preaches, "starve your distractions, feed your focus."

One thing that I have learned is that it's not our duty to do what those before us have already done, it's our duty to treat what they've built as a foundation for what we intend to build. Just like athletes have done in the pro sports that have been around much longer like basketball, football, baseball, etc. I laugh when people act like Kevin Durant wouldn't dominate like he does today if he played back when Rick Barry was shooting granny style.

I see all other professional athletes as my peers and equals. Yes, I realize that some are famous, rich and some of the most freakish people on the planet while I'm considered an undersized blocker at 6'5". But what intrigues me is what they're doing when none of that matters. These are the type of athletes that particularly fascinate me. Now that I have that same label as an American professional athlete, I look at these NBA, NFL, MLB athletes and what I'm curious about is how they think, how they train, their efficiency and leadership capabilities, etc. In all honesty, from what I've seen in my first six years of being a pro alongside these athletes, I'll take John Hyden's discipline up against the whole LA Lakers [post-Kobe, of course], Phil Dalhausser's freakish combination of physicality, finesse and confidence against any big man in the NBA, I'd rank April Ross's relentlessness in her individual pursuit of greatness right there with any male or female athlete at the 2017 ESPYs, and Kerri Walsh-Jennings's 4 olympic podiums (3 gold,1 bronze) over Usain Bolt's 8 gold medals (having 3 opportunities to medal each Olympics).

Fact is, I was raised to think this way. To love all sports and to enjoy all the small nuances of each one. My approach has become to take all the small things that I've learned from each sport I've played and apply it to being an elite athlete, not just a beach volleyball player. For example, I've learned a ton from the humbling nature of ocean sports, the teamwork aspects of basketball and indoor volleyball, the physical conditioning and endurance in soccer and outrigger canoe paddling, the mental game of golf, the balance of physicality and finesse of football and of course the ability to deal with the elements in sailing and surfing (wind, sun, rain, snow). The amazing sport of beach volleyball just so happens to be the perfect combination of all these things and more. Unlike indoor volleyball, beach volleyball is a sport that favors those who do not specialize in one aspect of athleticism. You need to be great at every aspect of the game and that's what I love about it.

I'm not sure what I'd be doing if I had never discovered beach volleyball upstairs on the baby court at Outrigger, but I'm very grateful to those before me who dedicated their lives to getting this sport to where it is today and for creating the opportunities for a kid from Hawaii to come up to the mainland and make a living as a professional beach volleyball player. We're very fortunate to have the opportunity to carry the torch as we do our best to give back to the next generation and to push the sport beyond anywhere it's ever been. I believe this sport will continue to grow to new levels, I see no reason to think otherwise.

Aloha.

INTRODUCTION

"I've never felt so happy, so alive, to be in so much pain."

In September of 2009, a man named Simon Sinek stood on a stage in Puget Sound, Washington, in front of a small crowd of big people, and spoke for 18 minutes in a now-famous speech that most refer to as "Start With Why," an eponym of a book he published a month earlier.

The speech has been viewed more than 5 million times. The book has been reviewed nearly 52,000 times on Goodreads with an average rating of 4.07 out of 5.

I have seen the speech several times. I have discussed the book with four-time Olympian Reid Priddy. I understand the message: In order to inspire great action, we must first understand why we're doing what it is we're doing.

Why is this important?

Why is this worth the time, effort, money, and emotional and physical strain we're investing to accomplish whatever it is we seek to accomplish?

Why?

It's Monday. May 14, 2018. Three days before the AVP Austin qualifier, which will begin with 64 teams, yet only four will make it out of the qualifying tournament and into that weekend's main draw.

My partner, Raffe Paulis, and I just finished up a practice against Ed Ratledge and Rafu Rodriguez, a pair of longtime pros. We played well, splitting two sets, winning the last, 21-15. A perfect tune up for what is surely to be a nasty qualifier on Thursday.

I've known Raffe for a while now. Two years prior, a week after having moved from the Gulf Coast of Florida to California, I played him in the AVP Huntington Beach qualifier in the first round.

He beat me and my buddy Matt Nelson 21-9, 21-16.

Understandably, it took two years of constant messaging to get him to just to practice with me. Though we had known each other for quite a bit, neither of us *really knew* the other. We had never had a conversation that went deeper than a brief analysis of the match we had just played or the tournament that was going on.

So it took me by surprise when, on our walk back to our cars, he asked me a question that dug a little deep: Why do I want to qualify? Do I really want it? Or do I just kind of want it?

I laughed. Hadn't he seen my writing? Hadn't he seen how much it hurt to lose in Hermosa Beach the year before? And in Huntington Beach just a week prior?

He had. But it still didn't answer the question: Why do I want to qualify?

We reached our cars.

I didn't have an answer. I stammered over a few. Something about being respected as an athlete. About proving to myself that, after a lifetime of playing sports, I had what it took to be a professional.

But those answers weren't it. I knew it. Raffe knew it.

And over the next week, my search for that answer proved to be the key to, for the first time, beginning to understand myself, and not just the beach volleyball player, but the human being, the son, the brother, the writer, the optimist, the grinder – it answered every piece of my deeply-layered identity.

That question helped me to find my why.

This book will examine the whys of others in their own pursuit of professional beach volleyball.

I'll begin with mine.

I've always admired athletes.

My father played quarterback for a high school in Pittsburgh and once beat Dan Marino. My mother, though the happiest woman you'll ever meet, is a ruthless competitor who still runs half-marathons despite more knee surgeries than I care to count. They met at Grove City College, and my dad fell in love the day he saw my mom chew out the left fielder on her softball team for flirting with a guy rather than fielding a fly ball. I loved hearing my dad regale stories of his football days, just as I loved hearing about my Uncle Jim Alcorn breaking every passing record there was to break in the state of Pennsylvania, how he tore it up in college and was on the God-blessed Browns for a brief period of time. I loved watching my cousin Dan play basketball at Robert Morris, and watching my other cousin, Matt, shoot under par on golf courses. I take immense pride in my other cousins, Claire and Jane, dominate as two-sport athletes at Marist College.

My favorite memories as a child came either on a playing field, in our driveway playing the made-up basketball games that children do, or at Baltimore Orioles games with my mom, dad, and two brothers.

When I watched the Orioles, my focus always turned to two players: Mike Mussina and Brady Anderson. Whenever I protested eating my vegetables, or showering after practice, or drinking milk, or getting in an extra hour of practice, my dad would say "Well Mike Mussina would…" and that was all the convincing I'd need.

If Mike Mussina did it, then I'd do it, because I wanted to be just like Mike Mussina one day. Whenever I played sports, I asked for No. 35, Muss's number. If 35 wasn't available I'd take 9, for Brady Anderson.

Because I was going to be like them one day. Just you watch.

I was going to be a professional athlete.

My ambition to become an athlete began long before I had ever stepped foot on a beach, before I had ever touched a volleyball, before I had accomplished anything of note.

But it did not answer the question of why.

I dug another layer deeper.

It's August of 2015. I've just had one of the most difficult conversations I've ever had in my life: I told my editor and good friend, Seth Stringer, that I'd be leaving the Northwest Florida Daily News.

He didn't understand why.

To be honest, at the time, and even two and a half years after, I didn't, either. I couldn't explain it to myself, so how could I possibly explain it to anyone else?

My life in Florida, on paper, was perfect, idyllic, damn near quixotic. I was writing for a paper I loved, in a town that I adored, for people and athletes I respected and rooted for, in the most beautiful part of the world I had ever seen, living with a wolf dog I adopted and subsequently became enamored with. I loved my boss. I loved my job. I loved my friends. I loved my life.

I was unhappy.

Well, perhaps unhappy isn't the word. If you've met me you know I'd probably be happy if I were hit by a dump truck and relocated to Siberia, so long as I have my brothers, dog, and a beer.

Anxious. Unfulfilled.

Yes, those words fit the bill.

I couldn't understand it. Just months before, I had won Sportswriter of the Year for the state of Florida for our circulation size, and shortly after was named second in the same category on a nationwide scale. I was enjoying more success and independence and freedom as a professional writer and human I had ever had.

So why was I so jittery?

Wasn't this what I had dreamed of since I began writing? Wasn't this exactly what I had worked for?

So why was I constantly looking for the next thing? The next mountain?

The next…what could possibly be next?

Was this it?

My mind jogged back to my favorite piece of literature, Teddy Roosevelt's 'Man in the Arena.' Though it is littered with countless gems, this is the one you're likely to know: *"It is not the critic who counts; not the man who points out how the strong man stumbles, or where the doer of deeds could have done them better. The credit belongs to the man who is actually in the arena, whose face is marred by dust and sweat and blood; who strives valiantly; who errs, who comes short again and again, because there is no effort without error and shortcoming; but who does actually strive to do the deeds; who knows great enthusiasms, the great devotions; who spends himself in a worthy cause; who at the best knows in the end the triumph of high achievement, and who at the worst, if he fails, at least fails while daring greatly, so that his place shall never be with those cold and timid souls who neither know victory nor defeat."*

I wish I had done this introspection when I was still living in Florida, for only now do I understand why I was so restless: I was no longer in an arena. I wasn't daring greatly.

I was coasting.

For some, this works, and I get that. My life was remarkably easy, consistent, comfortable. Enviable, even, depending on your perspective. But a line from Chip and Dan Heath in their book, The Power of Moments, kept replaying over and over and over again: *"We are most comfortable when things are certain, but we feel most alive when they're not."*

I had stopped feeling truly alive. The challenges had stopped, and when challenges stop, so, too, I've found, does your growth and learning. That feeling you get in your veins the night before a match, or a performance, or a speech – whatever your arena is – was dormant. I hadn't felt that electric pulse, those nervous-excitement butterflies, in quite some time.

I hadn't felt alive.

And if I wasn't growing, learning, feeling my pulse jump out of my neck from time to time, then what in the world was I doing?

I sent out some emails, made a few calls, and I got my answer.

I was moving to California.

But why?

I told everyone it was for writing. "Either have to move to LA or New York to make it as a sports writer!" I'd say, and everybody would believe me, because that's partially true, though I knew that wasn't quite it. I knew that beach volleyball played a large role in my decision to uproot my life for the second time in three years and move across the country.

And I knew that it was totally irrational, insane, ridiculous, inexplicable.

So I kept it to myself.

But in the midst of that irrational explanation, in the midst of the ridiculousness, I was, whether I knew it or not, beginning to find my why.

In beach volleyball, I had found something that made me feel truly, genuinely, wildly alive.

It's the second day of the 2018 season-opening event, Federation Internationale de Volleyball (FIVB) Huntington Beach. I'm on my way to interview Canada's top blocker, Sarah Pavan, who just beat the No. 1 American team, April Ross and Alix Klineman in three sets. John Mayer, one of best defenders in the United States, is leaving the player's tent, having just lost to Norway's young up-and-comers, Anders Mol and Christian Sorum.

Tough match, I tell him.

He shrugs, smiles, says that he and Trevor Crabb, his new blocker for the year, actually played their best match against them. Norway simply played better.

"Can't control the results."

The results from my match, against a different Norwegian team, were still haunting me. My partner, Skyler McCoy, and I lost, 15-13, in the third set, after leading 8-5 and 12-10. I couldn't sleep that night, replaying a line shot I hit out at 13-12 over and over and over again, replaying a lift, a missed block, a botched pass.

Can't control the results.

But here's what I can control: What I do with those results.

So I watched the film from that match for the hundredth time, and it was no less painful or wince-inducing. I noted what I did wrong, how to improve it. On Wednesday, the day before the Austin qualifier, I cobbled together four friends – Kevin Villela, Joel Blocksom, Zach Perry, Travis Woloson – and bribed them into serving me hundreds of balls. We did nothing but pass, set and side out for two hours, and in my head, every pass was me getting served at 13-12 in the third set.

Every. Single. One.

I'd never felt so dialed in for two hours of monotony.

Later that night, at a cheap hotel in Austin, I slept as well as I had in months.

I had done everything I could to prepare for the qualifier. You can't control the results. You can control your preparation.

The results take care of themselves.

And when you realize that, as I did in that creaky hotel room, you realize it's never been about the results. It's never been about qualifying.

It's about so, so, so much more.

One day later, it's 12-11 in the third set of the third round of 2018

AVP Austin. We're down to an up-and-comer in Eric Beranek and a legend in Matt Prosser. This is typically where my nerves begin to take over. Where I silently pray they serve my partner, so that if he doesn't side out – the volleyball term for scoring offensively – then I can, in my head, alleviate the blame for why I lost in the third round again.

The nerves don't come.

They don't come because I've done this drill before. Hundreds of times, actually. Just yesterday. I passed so many balls, sided out so many balls, in this exact scenario.

I've never been calmer in a high stakes situation.

I side out.

A few minutes later Raffe and I are hugging. We pulled it out, 16-14. We pulled it out despite being down in the third. Despite me blowing a 20-19 match point in the second.

We pulled it out in the exact spot where, only a week before, I had crumbled.

And then we did it again.

Down 5-2 in the third set of the final round to Dylan Maarek and Andrew Dentler, we rally. We rally despite getting smacked all over in the first set, 21-14. We rally despite me shanking one pass and getting called for an illegal set. We rally despite Maarek playing some of the finest volleyball I've ever seen him play.

We rally because I've been in this scenario before. Hundreds of times. Just yesterday at practice. The results are beginning to take care of themselves.

We push it to 11-11.

We score four straight.

We win.

We qualify.

We make a main draw.

Suddenly Raffe is jumping. He's screaming "TRAVIS" at the top of his lungs. I check the ball mark.

It's out?

Out.

No net?

No net.

We qualified?

We qualified.

I'm holding Raffe. Shaking hands. Hugging Dylan. Hugging Dentler. Hugging my good friend, Tri Bourne. Hugging refs.

I'm hugging goddamn everything.

It's 11 p.m. and six of us – Tri; Raffe; his girlfriend, Avery Bush; her incredible mother, Jill; and a professional player on the women's side, Delaney Knudsen; and I – are piled into one stinky, sweaty car.

"Smells like victory," Delaney says. I laugh, though I immediately regret it. My abs begin to cramp, which makes my lower back cramp, which makes my quads cramp.

I've never felt so happy, so alive, to be in so much pain.

The texts from the volleyball world pour in. My friend, Judd Smith, the one who initially taught me to play this game, calls me. He's crying. Says he loves me. Proud of me. I deserve it.

There are lots of exclamation points in every text and message I receive. Everyone is proud of me. So proud.

We arrive at the hotel and I take a quiet moment to myself outside, just to breathe for a second. I begin to see a common thread in those messages, every single one of which I screen-shotted and saved on my phone.

They'd have been proud of me whether I qualified or not.

Because it's not about the results. It's about what we can control. It's about the work you put in to get those results. I had put in my work. I had been vulnerable, exposed, open to failure. And they had seen every step of it, every shortcoming, every bounce back.

I smile. Let my head droop into my hands.

And everything – my admiration for Mike Mussina and Brady

Anderson and professional athletes, my restlessness in Florida, my masochistic habit of failing over and over and over again for reasons that were once unknown – slides into place.

Throughout the weekend, Raffe asks me close to a dozen times whether I'm stoked to qualify. I laugh every time. Yes, of course I'm stoked to achieve something I've been working towards for three years, 11 months and two days.

But I've come to see life as a series of false peaks. I talked to my pastor, Graeme Cowgill, about this. Every time we think we achieve our ultimate goal, that we reach our perceived peak, there's another one just up ahead, a taller mountain with a better view. Oftentimes, we're so focused on getting to that next peak that we forget to take a look and enjoy the view from this one.

I knew before Thursday, before that ball landed out, before AVP Tournament Director Jeff Conover shook my hand and welcomed me to the AVP Tour, that simply qualifying was a false peak. That there would be another one just beyond that, and another just beyond that. I've found that my happiness resides in the space between those peaks. And though we only stop to take pictures and breathe and enjoy it from the top of those peaks, our why resides in that uphill climb, where we learn and grow and discover who we truly are. That's where our hearts beat the loudest, where we stumble, bleed, bruise.

Where we get back up again.

I'm immensely proud for having qualified for the AVP Tour. But I'm far prouder for stepping back into the arena after heart-wrenching losses in Manhattan Beach, in San Francisco, in Huntington Beach. I'm far prouder for finding myself in the exact situation I'd buckled in Huntington and instead stayed calm and put the ball away. I'm proud for turning down jobs that College Travis, the one who majored in journalism at the University of Maryland and whose ambition it was to work at Sports Illustrated one day, would have considered dream jobs, jobs to cover Florida State, Florida, the Pittsburgh Steelers, the Denver Broncos, Tennessee. I'm proud because that means I didn't take the easy way out, that I stayed on the path that makes my heart go thump-thump. I'm proud of the discipline I've developed, waking up at 5 or 5:30 every morning to get in a practice or a lift. I'm proud of the vulnerability it takes to continually subject myself to losing and failing, and then digging deep into that failure to extract a learning moment, and improving from it. And I'm proud that I haven't lost myself amidst all of that, that I remain rooted, above all, in kindness, and that I still took the time to learn every ball girl's name and shook their hands afterwards and told them what an excellent job they did, because I know that's exactly what would have made my day as a child.

That right there.

That's my why.

I could have never known this as a child, but Little Travis admired Mike Mussina and Brady Anderson and his cousins and uncle and parents because he saw in them traits he wanted to develop. They were an amalgamation of who I wanted to become. And every day I step back into the arena, every time I take a failure and turn it into a positive, every time I accept a loss and don't lose my sportsmanship in spite of it, every time I don't hit the snooze button, every time I do the extra rep, I get closer to that person I'd have admired as a child.

I'll never get there, and that's the point.

That's my why. That's why I keep going, keep pushing.

Everybody in this sport has their own why. Money surely is not it. It took me just shy of four years to qualify for the AVP Tour. And on that blissful weekend in Austin, I made $1,000. I made $1,000 despite finishing 13th in the entire country – the entire country!

Four years. One-thousand bucks.

You'd have to be either courageous or certifiably insane to play this sport for the money. So no, this is not a book about a group of hedonists living the dream life west of the Pacific Coast Highway. It is not a book about the cozy lifestyle of professional athletes. This is a book about grungy hotel rooms and ramen noodles, about rubbing pennies together and sleeping in vans and under piers and the stars, about taking chances, about failing and failing and failing, over and over and over again, until you find a single moment to cling on, the one that makes it all worth it, the one that keeps you going, vindicating those failures as necessary lessons. It's about a sport that will grind you into the very sand upon which it is played, and it is about becoming entirely, totally, unequivocally enamored with doing so. It is about a group of bold, reckless individuals determined to put the norms of society at bay for just one more day, one more sunrise, one more tournament.

One more day at the beach.

AVP NEW ORLEANS

"Not like this. Oh, my God."

M ike Brunsting sat on the floor of his hotel room in New Orleans with his girlfriend and stillborn dreams.

The day hadn't yet reached noon.

Brunsting knew it wasn't going to be easy, knew the odds were astronomically against him. He had seen the qualifier bracket, recognized the names. There, at the bottom of his portion of the bracket – each qualifier bracket for a 16-team main draw is broken into four quadrants, with the winner of each quadrant earning a main draw berth – in the AVP New Orleans qualifier on April 13, the first tournament of the 2016 season, was Adam Roberts and Marty Lorenz. Roberts has been around the game almost as long as Brunsting has been able to walk, having played in his first AVP main draw in 1998. At the final stop of the 2016 season, in Chicago, he would stand amongst the legends – John Hyden and Todd Rogers, Phil Dalhausser and Nick Lucena – and laugh when he realized that he had played in more AVP events than any of them. Lorenz, Roberts's 25-year-old blocker, had finished third in Mason, Ohio, just a year before. A star in the making, if not one already. But Brunsting would only play against them if everything went perfectly, two matches down the road, where they would vie for a bid to an AVP main draw – far from a guarantee. Rain continued to fall in buckets from the charcoal New Orleans sky. The AVP, under mother nature's time constraint, was forced to truncate the games to 11, 11 and 7, as opposed to the traditional format of 21, 21, 15.

Anybody could beat anybody in a game to 11.

Single elimination. Lose 22 points and sorry, you're out. As far as volleyball goes, your trip to New Orleans is over. Go check out Bourbon Street and the French Quarter.

Brunsting looked at the names across his on the bracket: Jody Pigford and Brent Dilts. Local guys, Pigford a seasoned veteran who grew up playing on the circuits in South Florida, Dilts an anesthesiologist from Mississippi moonlighting as a beach volleyball player. Brunsting didn't know either of them. It can be scary, the unknown. No film. No known tendencies. Nothing.

"I don't know if I can beat this team," he thought. "Who are these guys?"

But then his partner, Chase Frishman, Brunsting's former teammate from their college days at the University of California, San Diego, playing in his first AVP event, ripped jump serves that "damn near knocked me over," Dilts would say afterwards. The match proved to be of little consequence, an 11-4, 11-5 smacking.

Just like that, the nerves were gone.

The second round was tougher, though not significantly so. They dropped Ohioans Jon Drake and Chris Luers in two sets, 11-8, 11-8. It was all a prelude to the highly-anticipated clash with Roberts and Lorenz, who had allowed a total of 23 points in their first two matches combined. Darkness, however, had set in, forcing the match to be played the next morning under the standard format: Two games to 21, a third to 15 if necessary.

"We show up thirty to forty minutes before the game," Frishman said. "Everyone had been there and lathered in sweat like they had been there for an hour and me and Mike were like 'Oh shit, we should have been here.'"

Where Frishman was all nerves and second-guessing, Brunsting was self-assured. Confident. He liked the way they matched up with Lorenz and Roberts. The bid was theirs for the taking.

"At this point I was pretty excited," Brunsting said. "I feel like, in hindsight, I don't know what Chase would say, but we were just so – we tried so, so hard to do everything right and just not play our game."

Whatever game they were playing, it was working. In the first set they led 20-19 and were receiving serve. Side out – the volleyball term for scoring offensively – for the win. Everything went as planned. They served "this lollipop serve" to Frishman. An easy pass to set. But when Brunsting went to set Frishman, his hands clammed up. The ball didn't enter his hands cleanly, nor did it leave cleanly, coming out in two contacts as opposed to one.

"Please," Brunsting thought as he let go of a set he knew would be called illegal. "Not like this. Oh, my God."

The ref whistled Brunsting for a double-contact (an illegal set), awarding the point to Lorenz and Roberts. The wheels came off from there. Brunsting and Frishman lost that set, 28-26. And then they lost the second, 21-19. Just like that, their New Orleans trip was over. They were not going to make the main draw. They were not going to make money. They were done.

"That was one of the toughest losses I've had because we were – we should have won," Brunsting said. "I don't know how else to say it."

Roberts and Lorenz would go on to finish seventh in the tournament, cashing in on nearly $4,000. Brunsting and Frishman went home with a hangover.

"A tough pill to swallow," Frishman said.

"I remember going to the hotel room and I was just so upset, sitting on the floor with my girlfriend, Nicole, just saying I can't afford to fly around the country – pay thousands of dollars to fly around the country – to double a ball and lose the first set," Brunsting said. "I can't afford that. That's not what I signed up for."

On the contrary, that is exactly what Brunsting signed up for. Every player who has ever played in an AVP qualifier, which is every single active player on the AVP Tour, knows this to be true.

Welcome, the AVP seemed to be telling Brunsting, to the qualifiers. Welcome to the AVP Tour.

In the four years since Donald Sun had taken over the AVP Tour, rescuing it from a 2010 bankruptcy, nothing of much significance had happened. Sure, the Tour had returned to TV sets at home, on NBC seven or eight Sundays out of the year, at an awkward time slot that typically competed with the PGA Tour – but Sun paid millions of dollars in purchasing that time slot.

Isn't it supposed to go the other way? The network paying the league for the rights to televise its competition?

Not with beach volleyball.

Sponsors, after witnessing bankruptcies fracture the sport in 1999 and 2010, had grown wary of the Tour. The companies with the deepest pockets had seen Miller Brewing Company and Jose Cuervo, among others, pull out in the late '90s, and Crocs and Nissan and myriad others do the same in the 2000s. Under Sun, who emphasized a slow growth of the tour, prize money justifiably plummeted from where it had been in the mid-2000s, and players have referred to the meager winnings as everything from "a complete joke" (Nick Lucena) to, simply, "you will never see a TV show called 'Beach Volleyball Cribs,'" (Stafford Slick). Sinjin Smith made well over $200,000 per season on prize money alone, and that was in the early 90s. In 2016, it took the top six players combined to eclipse that threshold.

And with the limited sponsors creating limited pools of prize money, there also came the brutal downsizing of the number of spots in an AVP tournament. In the 70s, 80s and 90s, when Karch Kiraly and Kent Steffes and Smith and Randy Stoklos were leading the tour, tournaments could be as large as 128 teams, 256 players. When the

Manhattan Beach Open debuted in 1960, you could simply sign up and play in a professional beach volleyball tournament. Congratulations! You're a main draw player!

"A lot of people would enter just to say 'I got to play against Jim Menges and Ron Von Hagen in the first round! I took a facial! It was awesome! We scored a point! We didn't lose 15-0, we lost 15-1!'" said Kiraly, who won a gold medal in the 1996 Olympics with Steffes and is widely considered to be the greatest player of all-time. "I didn't ever want to be like that. I didn't enter just to play against somebody, I wanted to enter to compete and to win matches but there was this cool thing about it being a massive tournament and essentially anything could come."

But as the Tour grew larger and beach volleyball became something of a phenomenon, there came a need for what is known as a qualifying tournament – more commonly referred to as a "qualifier." Initially, the need for a qualifier was only when the AVP began expanding to land-locked sites, such as Dallas or Phoenix or Boston. The court space was limited, sometimes to as little as six total courts. The field had to be trimmed somehow. Enter the qualifiers. Over the years, they have taken on various forms. Almost all of them are single-elimination, though there have been exceptions, such as the 2008 Manhattan Beach Open qualifier, which was double-elimination.

"That was just weird," recalled Chris Luers, who won his first match in that qualifier, lost his second – which would have earned him a berth into the main draw – to Billy Strickland and 2004 Olympian Dax Holdren, and then lost his third match – which also would have earned him a berth into the main draw.

But in the beginning, qualifiers were a last-resort, used only when absolutely necessary, when the field would have been too large to finish the tournament. On the natural beaches like Manhattan and Hermosa, the size of the field wasn't necessarily an issue. They'd simply use more courts, and more courts, and more courts – as many as needed until they had enough to finish a tournament at a reasonable pace. Space really isn't much of a problem in Manhattan Beach.

Soon, though, it wasn't about so much about space as it was principle. Did two bros who just wanted to get blown up by Menges and Von Hagen and then go party – or was it the other way around? – really deserve to be in a professional volleyball tournament? And so qualifiers, in an attempt to make beach volleyball like anything else in life, became a meritocracy. Put together enough good finishes, and you'd accumulate enough AVP points, which were earned based on your finishes in tournaments, to skip the qualifier and be seeded directly into the main draw. Until then, you had to qualify to prove your mettle.

Even so, the qualifying tournaments weren't entirely stressful ordeals. The majority of main draws were 64 teams, and the Manhattan Beach Open went north of that number. With the top 48 teams already seeded into the main draw, there wasn't a whole lot of talent left to slug it out in the qualifier.

In 1995, the AVP even attempted a new look at the qualifying system: It founded a new tour, the Wilson Qualifying Series, which was one part developmental, one part qualifier. Playing in the Wilson Qualifying Series would earn the players AVP points, which was nice, but there was another carrot at the end of the stick: Along with prize money, the top six finishers from the series were granted exemption from the AVP qualifiers for the following season.

The qualifying series was short-lived, disappearing after the 1998 season, never to be heard from again. But those who played on it loved it. Todd Rogers and Sean Scott, two of the greatest of their generation, began their careers on the qualifying series. Adam Roberts cut his teeth in beach volleyball on the series as well. But when the AVP went bankrupt in 1999, it took the series down with it. When the AVP returned in 2001 under Leonard Armato, the man who had initially helped found the tour in 1984, it did so with one Tour and one qualifying system: a qualifying tournament.

Under Armato, as the Tour boomed, the main draw remained large, and qualifiers, while inconvenient, weren't necessarily formidable tasks. The qualifying tournaments still featured mostly fringe talents. But when the economy tanked, sponsors pulled out, and another bankruptcy struck, the size of the main draws shrunk out of necessity, and the qualifiers became bigger and bigger, featuring names that many were accustomed to hearing on television or even Olympic broadcasts. They have, in fact, become such stress-inducing affairs that it's not uncommon for players to skip them entirely. It's simply not worth the anxiety.

In September of 2014, the AVP was set to host its final event of the season in Huntington Beach. Matt Olson and Kevin McColloch were slated to play together, as they had for four previous events that season, with mixed results: a seventh, two ninths and a thirteenth. When the initial seeding for the Huntington Beach Championships was released, they had locked up the twelfth and final main draw slot. No need to play in the qualifier, which would allow just four of 39 teams into the main draw.

Thank God they didn't have to do that.

The problem with the initial seeding, however, is that it is just that: initial. Nothing is set until two days prior to the qualifier, when registration closes and the brackets are drawn. So when the bracket was released a few days later, and Olson and McColloch had a dreaded "Q" next to their seed, signifying that they would have to play in the qualifier, their spirits took a precipitous dive.

Let the second guessing begin.

They had played in Atlantic City just the week before and didn't even win a set, eliminated in the quickest manner possible: two matches, four sets. All losses. See you later. Did they have it in them to grind through a qualifier, where they would have to win three matches in a row?

"I'm not dying to do it," McColloch told Olson. "What do you think?"

Olson wasn't dying to do it either.

They dropped out. Justlikethat.

Screw the qualifiers.

Of course, there is a bit more to the story. There is almost always more to the story. That season, the AVP had instated a rule that, to be eligible for the championships, players were required to play at least four tournaments with one partner. In the days leading up to the Huntington Beach Championships, three separate teams, for various and justifiable reasons, split up and shuffled partners. By rule, they shouldn't have been allowed to compete, as none of them had played four tournaments with their new partners. The AVP allowed all three in the tournament anyway, which booted McColloch and Olson out of the main draw and into the qualifier, should they have chosen to play in it.

"It wasn't really a protest, but if they were going to put us in the qualifier, we didn't want to go," McColloch said.

It might sound childish, almost petulant, for grown men to scoff at the idea of needing to qualify, to earn – or re-earn, in the cases of Olson and McColloch – their right to play on the AVP Tour, but it's also understandable. Nobody wants to play in the qualifiers. And in Olson's case, he had been there and done that many times through, having played in at least one main draw for 14 straight years. There had been a point, sure, when the prospect of playing in a qualifier was an exciting affair for Olson.

Those days were long gone.

A San Diego kid and the son of a pair of recreational beach volleyball players, the game was ubiquitous in the Olson household. The only hiatus he has ever really taken from the game was when he was an underclassman in high school and spent most of his free time surfing instead of playing volleyball. That was more than 20 years ago, and his surfing kick lasted about a year.

"Since that day, I never stopped," Olson said. "I just fell in love with it. It was all I wanted to do."

It was all he really did do. He played indoor on the club team at the University of Arizona, leading the Wildcats to a pair of national titles. And when he wasn't busy hoisting national championship trophies, he was on the beach. His debut on the AVP Tour came in 2000, as a 20-year-old with Sean Burke. By the fourth event in 2004, he had qualified for the main draw nine times, and that year, he would go on to beat future gold medalist Phil Dalhausser as well as future two-time Olympian Sean Rosenthal. More important than either milestone victory, however, was this: After four years of playing in the qualifiers, Olson had alas eclipsed the points threshold to where he no longer had to.

"It's a way different ball game," he said. "Main draw is the greatest thing ever. You've seen those guys; they show up like late- to mid-afternoon in the qualifier. They show up in their sponsored gear, hit around with their buddies, go grab dinner and go home. You feel like you should be there and you have a chance to go deep into a tournament."

That was Olson for the better part of the next decade. He won events in Australia. He won events in America, his first on the AVP Tour coming in Belmar, New Jersey, in 2008 with Kevin Wong. His winnings nearly doubled every year from 2004-2008, reaching a career high of $75,537.50 in 2008.

"I had a nice little run there," Olson said with his signature penchant for understatement.

Yet there were Olson and McColloch in September of 2014, one erstwhile star and another main draw regular, thrown back in the qualifier at the Huntington Beach Open. No thanks. We're good. See y'all later.

They dropped out.

"It sucks, dude," Olson said. "It's so different nowadays on Wednesday night thinking 'Oh shit, I gotta go through a qualifier.'"

"Some guys try their whole lives," Taylor Crabb, the 2016 AVP Defensive Player of the year, said. "And a lot of them never make it."

They are undeniably brutal rites of passage, qualifiers. And as Sun slowly – and responsibly – builds up the Tour, the amount of main draw teams must remain limited. Most feature just 16 teams, though Sun has expanded several stops to 24. The Manhattan Beach Open is the one annual exception, allowing 32 teams into the main draw, eight of which will come out of the qualifier. Aside from Manhattan, the tournament starred and highlighted by every American player every year, making it to the main draw has become something of a Sisyphean Task, and that is not lost on players in generations both old and new.

"Most of the ones I was trying to get into were 32-team draws," Olson admitted. "That was the norm. In 2008, 2009, 2010 there were more 32-team draws than 24. The numbers were huge. I remember playing in 2006 and there were 100 teams in the qualifier. Back in those days it was cheaper; it was on a Friday, not on a Thursday. It was a way bigger carrot at the end of the tunnel. Back in the day, Manhattan, it was a 48-team draw. There were cases where it was 64. The year I made the Manhattan final [in 2009] it was a 64-team draw and there was another 85 or 100 teams in the qualifier that weekend and they let in 16."

A simpler way of putting it is that the pond has shrunk, while the fish have remained approximately the same size. In 2016 alone, Ty Loomis, an AVP winner, was in the qualifiers. Marty Lorenz, a regular top-five finisher, was in the qualifiers. Avery Drost, a three-time semifinalist, was in the qualifiers. Olson, a two-time winner who had finished in the top 10 in more than 80 events, was in the qualifiers.

"It's hard to overstate the difficulty of automatically getting in a sixteen-team main draw by points," said Kevin Villela, who made main draw by way of a qualifier in the 2015 Manhattan Open. "Today, you have to have finished at least ninth in four out of your last five tournaments to even have a shot at the twelve seed [in the main draw]. So taking last in one main draw didn't get me out of the qualifier mind-set – I'm still far from that point."

Indeed. Villela played in six of seven AVP events in 2016 and didn't make it out of a single qualifier, though he did finish 17th on two separate occasions, in San Francisco and Seattle. He missed the main draw in Chicago, the season's final event, by losing in the third set in the second round, on extra points. Had he played during Olson's heyday, he'd have been in the main draw in every event.

"It's a reality check," said Robbie Page, a 7-foot blocker out of UCLA who was automatically in the main draw in the first six events of the 2015 season before being relegated to the qualifier for the season-ender in Huntington Beach. "I knew I never wanted to be in a qualifier again. They have a crazy vibe to them: single elimination, cut-throat tournament, and a long day in the heat of the sun. Playing (indoor) at UCLA was much more structured and you knew what to expect every day. You have played in the gym before, you've watched hours of film on the opponent and have a full scouting report memorized. The ability to be prepared helps to cut down on nerves. In a qualifier, you have almost no preparation. You might be playing a team who you've never heard of before that is improperly seeded, on a court that is un-level, thrown together the day before. Hectic.

"Being in the qualifier in Huntington Beach [of 2015] was just what I needed to finish that year, a reality check to prove that I deserved to be in the main draw. And yes, there were nerves. We won a crazy three-set match against Brad Lawson and Adam Roberts. I'm still just really pumped I survived that qualifier. It was great feeling, but honestly, I can't remember the details of the moment too much. I think I was looking forward ready for bigger and better things."

The trick, then, in moving on to those bigger and better things that Page alluded to, is to qualify. A lot. It's no easy task, to solidify yourself among the top 24 players in the country – and perhaps that's the point.

"It should be hard to get in," John Mayer, the 2015 AVP MVP, said. "We want the teams that get in to be serious. I have a ton of respect for guys who make it."

Few at the top of the AVP in 2016 had a more difficult road in regards to qualifying than Mayer, which was also almost entirely, and remarkably, voluntary. In 2005, Mayer qualified in six out of seven attempts with three different partners, the final of whom was Matt Prosser. Had they stuck together for the 2006 season, they would have automatically been in the main draw via points, which are accrued at each tournament you play. The higher the finish, the more points you get, and the better seed you get. Earn enough points, climb the rankings, and you could be slotted directly into the main draw. But then Mayer did what, at the time, could have been viewed as unthinkable, though in retrospect was a savvy and prescient move: He picked up Brad Keenan, who had exactly zero AVP points to his name.

Back into the qualifier Mayer went.

The two had been indoor teammates at Pepperdine, and Mayer knew Keenan could play. It was just a matter of time before his indoor game translated onto the beach, which requires a more versatile, athletic skill set. Players cannot specialize on the beach as they do in indoor. They must be able to pass, set and side out, whereas in indoor, a player could, say, only be required to pass and play defense.

"I looked at Brad as an investment for the future," Mayer said.

Like many investments, the returns weren't immediately evident. They lost in the final qualifying round in their first tournament together in 2006, in Fort Lauderdale, Fla., and then whiffed again one month later in Tempe, Ariz. Though frustrated, Mayer never once considered dropping Keenan for a partner with enough points to pull him into the main draw, a practice that has since become commonplace on Tour.

"Sure, I could have played with this guy or that guy and been main draw, but the highest I could have probably finished with them was like seventeenth or thirteenth," Mayer recalled. "Money wasn't why I was doing it. I wanted to win a tournament, I wanted to be great. I saw someone with the ability to win and be great. I knew the payoffs would be there. It wasn't like I was wondering if he could do it. If it had been more unclear if Brad didn't have the skill set – it was more like once he gets the experience, we'll be good. There were some frustrating moments but I was pretty early in my career and I knew I had a long way to go. I wasn't good enough to be pointing fingers or anything. I wasn't in this for a quick fix."

As Mayer knew it would, his investment in Keenan paid off. They wouldn't miss a main draw again, even coming out of the qualifier to finish third in Hermosa Beach in 2006, which remains tied, through 2016, as the best main draw finish of any male qualifying team. But that was, justifiably, the last qualifying Mayer ever wanted to do. In May of 2016, he ventured out to watch the qualifying tournament prior to the Huntington Beach Open. He saw talents like Matt Olson and McColloch, Ed Ratledge and Ty Loomis populating the bracket. He felt no envy for them.

"I was just checking out the level, thinking 'Wow, there's a lot of athletes here that are bigger and faster than me,'" Mayer said. "It's cool to see the level high and that's the way it should be."

There is one enviable athlete who has never won a single set in an AVP qualifier, yet has managed to nearly avoid them altogether: Tri Bourne. His lone AVP qualifier came in August of 2012, in Cincinnati. Bourne was playing with a defender from Chicago named Raffe Paulis, who had made three main draws on the Jose Cuervo Pro Beach Volleyball Series, a second-tier domestic tour. The two were young, raw, athletic and brimming with promise.

They didn't even win a set.

Four years later, Paulis is still in and out of the qualifiers. Bourne is an AVP sensation.

Born in Honolulu, Hawaii, Bourne, the son of two P.E. teachers, his first name both an eponym of their love for triathlons as well as his status as the third child in the family, was essentially raised at the Outrigger Canoe Club, which is tenuously credited as the birthplace of beach volleyball.

"It was my daycare, basically," he said. "All of our families just kind of live out of the club. I paddled for the club and I did summer fun at the club and there's courts and a lot of people were good college players or really good college players and basically the parents of all my friends were good players – it just kind of naturally happened. There's just so many good volleyball parents and they get you into it. It wasn't serious, which is what I kind of loved about it. We just played and paddled and we just played beach for fun."

Only, with such a diluted talent pool, Bourne, something of a late bloomer in the volleyball world, was a small fish in a small pond filled with massive fish. From 2006-2016, Outrigger produced eight of the No. 1 volleyball recruits in the country. Bourne, who was talented but not to the level of some of his Hawaiian counterparts, like Riley McKibbin and Spencer McLaughlin, was overlooked, recruited by precisely one school, USC, who only agreed to look at Bourne because McKibbin, the No. 1 setter in the nation at the time, asked the coaches to do so.

"The coaches came down to watch me play and I told them 'Don't come watch me play, I'm already going there. Watch my buddy play, Tri Bourne,'" McKibbin recalled. "He was a middle blocker on his club team so nobody really gave him a look. But he was an outside on his high school team, and when they saw him they said 'Holy shit, who's this guy?'"

Bourne was offered a scholarship that night, and for the next four years, he and McKibbin roomed together, leading the Trojans to a national championship berth in 2010 and a third-place finish in 2011. After graduating, their paths diverged, as Bourne went overseas to play indoor volleyball professionally in Puerto Rico and Turkey while McKibbin signed to play in Italy.

"It was a really good experience, just the culture of it, training in Puerto Rico was really cool. It was awesome, but once I figured out that beach was a legit option, I was just like 'I'm over indoor,'" Bourne said.

He had actually planned to return overseas to play indoor, "just to make some money," he said, but he took half the season off to play on a beach tour in New Zealand with Will Montgomery, a former libero at the University of California, Irvine. That half season on the beaches of New Zealand with Montgomery was all it took to convince Bourne that he was meant to play on the sand. Bourne returned to the States in 2012, when Jose Cuervo was running the pro beach circuit and the AVP was attempting to revive itself under Sun. While they technically weren't AVP events, it is worth noting that Bourne did play in a handful of Cuervo events in which he did have to qualify, in a qualifying tournament that mirrored the single-elimination style of the AVP. He made the main draw in his second attempt, in Belmar, New Jersey with Jeff Carlson. And it would be easy to point to that event as evidence of providence of some kind, of a higher power governing destinies. Because Bourne and Carlson, in the first round, matched up with the top seed of John Hyden and Everett Matthews, the two men who would, one year later, begin developing Bourne into one of the most formidable blockers in the world.

It was not, however, the obvious transition it appears to be. If this were a movie, Hyden would have noticed the unbelievable raw talent in front of him and immediately picked up Bourne as a partner, and the two would go onto become one of the best teams on the planet. But this is not a movie. And that is not how it went. Not at first.

"I honestly don't think I remembered [Bourne]," Hyden said, despite him and Matthews actually losing to Bourne and Carlson that day. "I was playing with Evee, and he doesn't block, and I don't really block. If Sean [Scott, Hyden's regular partner], had been playing, I think that match would have gone a bit differently. We would have taken care of them."

There is little doubting that. In 2011, Corona sponsored a tour called the Wide Open Series, which had been founded by Karch Kiraly and featured the old school, side out scoring format and a bigger court. There were five total events. Hyden and Scott won all five. That same year, Jose Cuervo had also reentered the professional beach volleyball market with its Pro Beach Series. Hyden and Scott won two of three, and they also claimed the debut tournament of the upstart National Volleyball League, thumping Billy Allen and Matt Prosser in consecutive sets, 21-16, 21-15. The two were likened to the Baltimore Ravens defensive duo of Ray Lewis and Ed Reed. Scott, who stands 6-foot-5 and, fittingly, built like a middle linebacker, was the Lewis of the duo. Hyden, a crafty and cerebral defender, was Reed.

"Once you find the perfect fit, it just kind of rolls from there," Hyden said.

For three years, the good times rolled for the two, winning 19 tournaments on a menagerie of tours between 2009 and 2012. But in 2012, when the AVP was undergoing a restructuring under Sun's new ownership, the money had dried up. Scott had a newborn child and a family to care for, and when USA Volleyball offered him a job to be the director of the national beach programs, the choice seemed obvious.

"A lot of people were upset with him but I wasn't one of them," Hyden said. "For me, I had more to do. I was at a loss. I didn't know what to do. I didn't have an option. I didn't know who I was going to play with."

When Scott, who was raised in Kailua, Hawaii, retired, he had an idea: What about that wiry kid from Honolulu whom Hyden had met a few months before, at a Cuervo stop in Belmar? What about Tri Bourne?

Hyden shrugged.

Scott passed along Hyden's phone number to Bourne anyway.

"I hit up John, and I didn't think he'd pick me up or anything, but I'm obviously trying hard and working hard to impress him, and I'm talking like I know the game," Bourne said.

Bourne thought he had made a good impression. Hyden didn't even know the kid's name.

"I thought it was Tree," he said.

Regardless, Bourne had shown glimpses of what Hyden was looking for. In Bourne, who, like Scott, stands 6-foot-5, Hyden saw semblances of his former partner.

"I played with him and talked to him a little bit and I could see he was a lot like Sean in some ways. He was really athletic but he was really raw," Hyden said. "He had no coaching. I felt like I could mold him into doing stuff Sean would do. And it kind of just – I felt like I could take a chance on him."

"One day he just told me 'I'm down to give this a shot,'" Bourne recalled. "And I was like 'What? I didn't know that was a legit option. I will drop everything.' So I basically made a commitment to be a full-time professional athlete right then."

"Afterwards, he tells me 'Man, I was so nervous those first few days,'" Hyden said. "I thought that was pretty funny."

In Bourne, Hyden had found the second coming of Scott, a lanky, wildly athletic Hawaiian blocker. In Hyden, Bourne had found his golden ticket to the AVP Tour: He would never have to qualify for a single AVP tournament.

"I honestly don't think there's a better partner for me in the world, on the world tour, AVP, anything," Bourne said. "I will say I did put in a decent amount of work. It was kind of behind the scenes though, you know? We had little open tournaments and we were able to beat decent players, even Kevin Wong when he came home. And I did the New Zealand tour that nobody else saw.

"But yea, I got so lucky, and I was super grateful for it. But part of me is kind of like, 'It's meant to be.' Playing indoors, I took an oath that

I love being a professional athlete, so I'm going to do everything I can to continue being a professional athlete, training right, dieting right, just looking to do everything the right way. And that's what he was looking for: 'Who's going to put in the work I am going to put in?' He's not just going to pick up some young guy who's screwing around. When you're his age, you can't have that. So I think it was kind of meant to be."

Hyden and Bourne made their AVP debut in 2013 in Salt Lake City. It was Bourne's first main draw appearance on the AVP Tour, though he wouldn't show it. In his second match, he beat 2008 gold medalist Todd Rogers and his 7-foot blocker, Ryan Doherty. By tournament's end, he and Hyden would take fifth. It wasn't a finish befitting the Hyden-Scott era, but it was a start.

"I was nervous in a good way, you know?" Bourne said. "If it means enough to you, you're going to be nervous about it. It wasn't overwhelming. I think, playing [overseas] indoor, you basically have to put the team on your back or you'll get fired and the town won't like you. So the pressure on the beach wasn't bad; I just knew I had to get out and prove myself."

On American soil, Bourne proved that Hyden's decision to pick him up in the wake of Scott's retirement was a prescient one. In 2013, their first season together, they played in seven tournaments, placing in the top five in six of them while making back-to-back finals in Santa Barbara and Huntington Beach. Bourne's transition from qualifier to consecutive finalist earned him AVP Rookie of the Year and Most Improved Player. But still, Bourne had "a little chip on my shoulder," he said. "I had watched a lot of those guys and they don't want some kid coming up and beating them. It's almost like an initiation."

His unofficial initiation came in the second event of the 2014 season, in Milwaukee, when Bourne and Hyden took down Olympians Phil Dalhausser and Sean Rosenthal in the finals, 21-15, 21-18, for Bourne's first AVP win. Of the six matches the two played, four went to three sets, and four included either Olympians at the time or Olympians in the future.

"It was unreal," he said. "That was kind of – as a beach volleyball player, you kind of dream about winning an AVP tournament. I think some people get wins on their resume in smaller events but to know that you beat Sean Rosenthal and Phil Dalhausser in a stacked AVP – that was unreal. That solidified in my head that this was a reality. You got to get one first to know that you're ever going to win."

And win Bourne would. In 2014, Bourne and Hyden made the semifinals in six out of seven tournaments, winning in Milwaukee and placing second in Huntington Beach. In 2015, despite playing the majority of the season overseas in an attempt to qualify for the 2016 Olympics, he and Hyden won back-to-back AVP tournaments to finish the AVP season, the first in Mason, Ohio, the second in Huntington Beach, Calif. Their worst finish the entire year, in four AVP tournaments, was third.

"Now, it's kind of fun because I'm looking eye to eye with the legends of the sport," he said. "And I'm still ten years younger than pretty much all of them."

It is easy to be envious of Bourne's overnight success. Very few in the game, particularly with the 16-team format many main draws have adopted, can say they have only needed to play a single qualifier before blossoming into an AVP phenomenon. But Bourne, and anyone who is close to him, will note that it was not handed to him, that while, yes, he was picked up by one of the best players in U.S. beach volleyball history, he earned every last point.

"The kid's a star," Jake Gibb, a three-time Olympian, said. "No question."

While Bourne is an exception, he is no exception to the actual rules of volleyball, that one must earn enough points to qualify for a main draw, and then maintain enough points to remain above that threshold.

Theo Brunner, among a few others, is the rare exception.

★ ★ ★

Theo Brunner was never supposed to play volleyball again.

Doctors had told him so. His heart, which an echocardiogram revealed had been suffering from a birth defect for more than 20 years, couldn't hold up under the stresses of volleyball any longer. He was done, and news spread like contagion to all of the professional indoor teams in Europe, including his own, which cut him on the spot. He was untouchable. Paradoxically, that was exactly why, on August 15, 2013, he had received a rare golden ticket from the AVP Tour: a wild card berth into the season-opening event of 2013, in Salt Lake City, Utah.

Wild cards are a hazy matter, entirely subjective and up to the whims of the tournament director. Mainly, though, they are reserved for medical exemptions and stars who still have the pull to attract fans but not enough points to make main draw. Should the now-retired Todd Rogers, for instance, attempt a comeback, rest assured you will not find The Professor in a qualifier. Brunner, however, was not Todd Rogers, though it was that very man who, in 2003, took a blind chance on the 6-foot-7 kid from Ridgefield, Connecticut, offering him a preferred walk on spot to UC Santa Barbara, where Rogers was an assistant, based on nothing but grainy footage of Brunner playing basketball – sent in from Brunner's mother.

"His recruiting tape started off with basically a minute of crazy basketball dunks, and I was like 'Holy crap! This kid gets up! Does he actually play volleyball?'" Rogers recalled.

Brunner had played volleyball. Sort of. Ridgefield High School started a team when he was a freshman, but it was so disorganized that Brunner didn't even have a position.

"We just kind of rotated around," he said, laughing.

During the summer following his junior year, Brunner got his first real taste of the sport, at a camp at Penn State, which at the time was in the midst of the most dominant run in womens college volleyball history, one in which it would win 1,187 matches to just 186 losses from 1979-2015. Brunner was a bit out of place.

"People were on the ground, like diving for balls and I was like 'What the hell is going on here? Why are people hurting themselves diving for a volleyball?'" Brunner recalled, laughing. "That was my first taste."

But even with virtually no experience, even with a recruiting video shot and emailed by his mother, Sally, it was not difficult to discern that Brunner was a hell of an athlete.

"He did some things, like hitting a ball from the ten-foot line, and I was like 'Whoa, this guy is a pretty good athlete,'" Rogers said. "So I went up to the coach, Ken Preston, and I said 'This kid is a walk on or a lower-level scholarship. He's not going to come in and be immediately gnarly but athletically, he's gnarly, and if we develop him he can be really good.'"

When Rogers offered Brunner a spot at Santa Barbara, Brunner was predictably thrilled. His parents were terrified.

"My parents thought it was a bad idea for me to go out there because my dad had a mythical perspective of California volleyball players and didn't think I'd make the team," Brunner said.

He went anyway, and he did make the team, though it was a bit of a shock transitioning from a team with no set positions to one where kids had been playing since they could walk. Brunner, being the exceptional athlete he was, had the talent to play anywhere with proper coaching. Not knowing any better, Brunner opted for the most simplistic, unsung position in volleyball: middle blocker.

"I didn't know any better," Brunner said. "I had beach in the back of my mind because of that reason, because the best I could be was be good at half the game because I was in the middle."

Brunner has mastered the art of understatement. Despite being good "at half of the game," and despite being thrown into a culture in which he felt out of place because his teammates and opponents were far more polished, he set the UCSB record for hitting percentage in his redshirt freshman year. The next season, he played in every game, the only Gaucho to do so. The next, he became an All-American. And even then, even after surpassing his teammates who were born and bred to play volleyball, even after proving he was worth far more than a pre-ferred walk-on spot, he wasn't sold on the indoor version of the sport. He liked it, and was a tremendous talent, but during breaks at Santa Barbara, he and a few teammates would head to the beach, running the CBVA circuit. Brunner played mostly with Gaucho libero Ben Brockman, and in 2006, after their sophomore seasons had come to a close, they even signed up for an AVP qualifier – and promptly forgot about it and didn't show up.

Whoops.

On only four other occasions would Brunner fail to qualify for an AVP tournament. He knew the beach was the path he wanted to take.

"It was like 'I could make a lifestyle out of this. This is pretty awe-some, just going to the beach,'" he said. "Especially a Connecticut kid it's like 'Oh, I get to spend the whole day at the beach and play volley-ball. That's a thing?' It's awesome. It never gets old. Never."

And yet he didn't play. Not full-time at least. There were offers in Italy to play indoor. There was guaranteed money. He loved the beach, sure. He also loved eating and having shelter and fulfilling Maslow's hierarchy of the most basic human needs, of which the beach offered none. To Italy he went.

During the indoor off-season, he'd return to California and play whatever AVP events happened to be on the schedule when he was in town, qualifying five times in 2009 and another three in 2010, bank-ing an extra $3,800. Then it was back to Italy. Back to the gyms and blocking and five teammates on the court as opposed to one. Back to medical exams. Back to – hold on for one second, Mr. Brunner, the echocardiogram just showed a defect in the heart. No more volleyball for you. No, sir.

Just like that, Brunner was cut. No severance. Just a plane ticket and a "sorry, your career is over."

Hope you studied in college.

He certainly did after. Brunner's volleyball career crash-landed in Connecticut, living with his parents. He studied for the GMAT and passed, began working towards an MBA he preferred not to have to use, took a job at a life insurance company he didn't want, saw a bunch of doctors he didn't want to see. Except one doctor took a look at Brunner and said he was fine. Sure, he could play volleyball. So long as Brunner checked in every year, he didn't see why not. One day in the life insurance business was enough for Brunner. He quit, began looking for contracts overseas. Nobody would touch him. Brunner was blacklisted.

"Everyone knew about my heart," he said.

And everyone in the States knew his heart was cleared by American doctors. Brunner scored an invite to train with the United States National Team.

Now he was back in Southern California, living in an apartment in Anaheim, courtesy of USA Volleyball, seeing all the familiar faces: Casey Patterson, Jake Gibb, Nick Lucena, Dave McKienzie. He should have loved it. He hated it. Too many middle blockers. Too much being indoors.

"I was looking for an out," he said.

McKienzie, a defender from Littleton, Colorado who liked Brunner's size and blocking, gave him one. There was a National Volleyball League event coming up in Dallas. Would Brunner want to play?

"Hell yea," Brunner said. "Let's fucking do it."

They did, and they took third. All the while, Lucena, one of the top defenders in the country who had just barely missed the 2012 Olympics, was watching.

"I thought he was physically one of the best blockers I've ever seen," Lucena said. "And I think he could be the best blocker the world has ever seen."

But Lucena was still set to play the season with Steve Grotowski, who competed in the 2012 Olympics for England. They set up a practice, Lucena and Grotowski vs. Brunner and "I don't remember who the other guy was," Lucena said, "but Theo blocked Steve like twenty-five times in a dang practice, and right then and there I said 'Steve, you're out.'"

A few days later, "Nick was like 'Let's fucking do it. Let's play in all the AVPs,'" Brunner recalled. "So I just quit the indoor team immediately and played that season with Nick. I was just like 'Shit, this is the best opportunity I'm going to get to play beach. I'm going to quit playing indoor and go for it.'"

One tricky problem: Brunner had zero AVP points. They would have to be in the qualifier, unless…

Wild card.

They applied for a wild card for their first event as a team, in Salt Lake City, using Brunner's medical condition and Lucena's clout as their chief arguments. The AVP obliged. Just like that, Brunner had skipped the qualifier, instead earning the nine seed. With a berth straight into the main draw, they tore through the bracket, nearly stunning Phil Dalhausser and Sean Rosenthal in the second round before clawing all the way back through the contenders bracket and into the semifinals, where, again, they'd meet Dalhausser and Rosenthal. They lost, 14-21, 20-22, but in placing third, they took home a momentous victory: Brunner now had enough points where a wild card bid was no longer necessary to qualify. Brunner, despite taking nearly two years off the AVP Tour, despite considering retirement, was a main draw beach volleyball player.

"I guess you can say I'm a little spoiled," he said.

Those relegated to the qualifiers are not.

In New Orleans in 2016, the only qualifying team to win a main draw match was Marty Lorenz and Adam Roberts. The remaining three teams out of the qualifier – Adam Cabbage and Alejandro Parra, Ty

Loomis and Ed Ratledge, Skylar delSol and Raffe Paulis – were knocked out in consecutive matches.

Because the only thing more difficult than qualifying for a main draw is perhaps winning a match once you're in it.

AVP HUNTINGTON BEACH

"And then we got our bell rung."

The foam in Mike Brunsting's beer hadn't even settled when he declared it: He wanted Casey Patterson.

The 24-year-old was fresh off the biggest victory of his life, a straight-set demolition of Ed Ratledge and Ty Loomis to qualify for the Huntington Beach Open. It was Brunsting's first main draw appearance in more than two years, and his partner Chase Frishman's first ever. Yet there was no reveling in the moment. No appreciating the size of their accomplishment, becoming one of the top 16 teams in the country.

Screw that.

They wanted Casey Patterson.

"Maybe," Frishman said, laughing at the memory, "we should have been a little more grateful for the moment."

Perhaps. Though it's difficult to blame them for riding so high in the wake of a day that was so dominant, so unbelievably smooth, that they hadn't even gone to a third set. Both were deemed, that day, to be on a path of expedited stardom, to the point that Taylor Crabb, who would be voted the AVP's best defender at season's end, dubbed Frishman "one of the best in the nation." And aside from Taylor and his brother, Trevor, there was no team with a more loyal, demonstrative following than Frishman and Brunsting, which was made patently clear in the final round of the Huntington Beach qualifier, where Frishman and Brunsting met Ratledge and Loomis. When Ratledge, who has passed thousands, if not millions, of float serves – a serve that has no spin, creating a knuckleball effect – in his life, shanked one into the crowd in the first set, that's when Frishman knew: This was their match. Anyone sitting in that crowd of rowdy, drunk, post-college 20-somethings who now had enough money to buy alcohol but not yet the responsibilities to really care about getting wasted by noon on a Thursday, knew this had been Frishman's and Brunsting's match from the very first point. With each serve, each set, each point, the crowd, mostly former Long Beach State indoor players, erupted like their boys had just qualified. They screamed out "LEDGE!" when Frishman dug a ball – "ledge," of course, being a reference to "legend," a nickname bestowed upon Frishman because "when you watch him play," Brunsting said, "he just looks like a legend." And did the kid – the legend – dig balls that day.

Loomis and Ratledge couldn't put anything down. High line? Frishman would chase it down and side out. Swing at him? He'd flip it up no problem.

What else ya got?

Soon the score was 10-4, then 14-7, then 18-10 – 21-13 by the time the first set was said and done.

"At that point, you're not in the AVP yet, you don't know if you can beat them, but I know Ty and Ed and we had trained against them, and we knew we could beat them," Frishman said. "It's not like we were playing them for the first time. It's trying to hold down the emotions, like 'Ok it's a big moment, they've been here before, we need to stay in the moment.'"

Frishman and Brunsting did. Ratledge and Loomis did not. It began with Loomis trying to go over on two – typically, in volleyball, there will be a pass, set, and hit; on occasion, the offense will attempt to score on its second touch to catch the defense off guard or out of position – futile attempts that Frishman would thwart with ease and flip them into easy points. And then Ratledge began passing balls all over the court – and also well off it. And then Loomis, whose volatile emotions have earned a reputation of their own, began jabbering with the raucous crowd, which was heavily in favor of the two rookies.

"That's some junior varsity bull shit," he sneered, and the crowd would only get louder, and the score would only lean more heavily in the favor of Frishman and Brunsting.

"I am only human," Brunsting said. "It was 18-12 or 17-11 and Chase and I kept looking back and forth saying 'Ok, this point!' 'Ok, this point!' 'Ok, get this!' It was weird how much we were taking it one point at a time, but we both knew it was very real. And Ty was starting to talk back to the fans which is a definite no-no. With four or five points to go, I think I realized it and got pretty excited."

They won the second set, 21-12, marking their most comfortable win of all three matches they played that day. In Frishman's second career qualifier he made the main draw. It had been 596 days since Brunsting had last qualified. They celebrated, swigging liquid out of bottles in brown paper bags, cheersing beers, hugging friends, kissing girlfriends.

And then they turned to Casey Patterson.

If he wasn't the best player on the AVP Tour, he was close. After he and Jake Gibb had partnered up following the 2012 Olympics, in which Sean Rosenthal dumped Gibb for Phil Dalhausser and Gibb subsequently turned to Patterson, the two had claimed the AVP Tour as their own. They won 10 tournaments in three years, seven more than any other team. In 2013, they made at least the semifinals in every single tournament, and finished the season having won four straight titles and 16 consecutive matches. Patterson led the AVP in kills per set (8.05) and kill percentage (.475). The next season they won three straight to finish tops on Tour again and in 2015 they added another two titles to the belt.

And if Patterson wasn't the best American player, he was unanimously, unquestionably the loudest.

In New Orleans in 2015, the AVP interviewed every player and asked for a fun fact about a former partner. Patterson, who had partnered with

Ryan Doherty in 2011 and stunned the beach volleyball world when they took down Dalhausser and Todd Rogers in a National Volleyball League final, had an unlimited amount of quirks and factoids to mention about Doherty. He could have mentioned that Doherty, at 7-foot-1 and a former pitcher in the Arizona Diamondbacks' system, was the tallest pitcher in MLB history; or how his California adventure began as a pizza boy; or how he used to hit jump serves by himself at practice, or how he had written a book. Patterson, of course, chose none of that.

"Ryan Doherty," he said to the cameras, "hasn't won a tournament since he dropped me" as a partner. And then he let out a long laugh and a smirk.

Thanks, Casey. Got it. Of course, what could you really say to Patterson after he won the tournament that year and knocked out Doherty in the semifinals?

"Casey is a loud guy, very demonstrative, I guess is the nice way of saying cocky, right?" Frishman said. "We love Casey, but we were fired up to prove that we weren't there just to be the fifteen seed in the tournament."

Every player on Tour is always fired up at the opportunity to beat Patterson, and with good reason, though Brunsting and Frishman had an extra "chip our shoulders," Frishman said. After their near-breakout performance in New Orleans just two weeks prior, Frishman and Brunsting had proven enough to be worthy of Patterson and Gibb's "training dummies," as Frishman called themselves. Whereas most of the top players lived north, near Los Angeles, Patterson and Gibb trained in Huntington Beach. Frishman and Brunsting, who lived in nearby Laguna Beach and Lake Forest, respectively, were deemed good enough to join their training group.

"Casey, whenever you train with him, all he does is talk shit, just eye roll after eye roll, and of course we're just the grunts he trains against," Brunsting said. "Like Chase would go up to hit a cut shot or a swing and Casey will mumble 'That's not realistic!'"

So when their main draw match against Patterson and Gibb began, they carried with them no small amount of animosity towards the voluble Patterson.

"We were fired up to prove that we weren't there just to be the fifteen seed in the tournament," Frishman said. "And then we got our bell rung."

The match was over in 33 minutes. Frishman and Brunsting scored a combined 23 points.

"Looking back on it," Frishman said, "if we had just been a little happier to be there and stayed in the moment – but I had been envisioning that moment, I believed I should be there, but I put the cart in front of the horse, so to say, thinking I should beat them right there. They were the better team and they still are and that's the truth of it."

The truth of it is that every team automatically in the main draw is better than every team in the qualifier. It's an undeniable fact of beach volleyball. A qualifying team will enter its first-round match with, statistically speaking, roughly an 11 percent chance to win. Since the AVP's restructuring in 2012 through the 2016 season, under the new ownership of Donald Sun, qualifying teams have won just 12 matches and 45 sets against the top-eight seeded teams in the first round, losing 101 matches and 220 sets, respectively. In 2015, qualifying teams went 0-32 in the first round, and it has been two years since a qualifying team won a single set in the first round of the Manhattan Beach Open. It's not exactly the warmest of welcomes to the AVP Tour. There is no celebratory banquet, no "congratulations! You've made it!" The first round is, simply, a baptism by fire.

"I love being the dark horse because nobody expects you to win," said Jon Mesko, who went just 1-13 in AVP first round matches after coming out of the qualifier, and that lone win came after playing just one match in the preceding qualifier. "So when you first qualify it's pretty much like winning a tournament, and you celebrate, and then you come back the next morning, you go into that tournament thinking you have nothing to lose. You're predicted to lose."

Which is not the same thing as saying you expect yourself to lose.

In 2006 and 2007, Aaron Wexler had played in every single qualifier. He had also lost in every single one of them. His beach volleyball dream was fueled with day shifts waiting tables at Duke's, a restaurant in Malibu, and odd catering jobs. Wexler celebrated when he made $100 a shift, refusing to put his environmental science degree from UCLA to use and accept a sit-down job because he "had to get my training in, man."

For hundreds of days, he had beat the sun to the beach for early morning practices and stayed out long after it left during his evening session. Financially, he was broke. Spiritually, he was exhausted. But in June of 2008, in Hermosa Beach, Wexler, playing alongside 6-foot-3 Venice native Travis Schoonover, was sitting in the angle on defense against A.J. Mihalic and Scott Davenport, the number one seed in the qualifier, and he watched as Mihalic blasted a swing "like three inches out of bounds" in the third set of the final round.

At long last, Wexler had done it: He made an AVP main draw.

"Man, pure bliss just to qualify," Wexler said. "And you know all qualifiers, they're hard, they're dog fights. Just to win that first match is great, but to win three to get in? Man, that's tough. Our first two matches were good, and that third match was a grinder. It went three, back and forth, everyone was tired, late in the day, and I'll never forget it. I didn't have the legs, I was getting served every ball, I wasn't passing very well, a lot of shanks, but I just stuck with it and I remember it was pure bliss, qualifying, making that dream happen of getting in. Any beach volleyball player wants to make main draw. Before you talk about winning, you just want to make it."

And here was his reward: The first thing the next morning, he and Schoonover were going to play against Phil Dalhausser and Todd Rogers, the number one team on the planet.

"It's funny, thinking back eight years ago, and thinking back on that emotion, I can still feel that raw emotion right now, just total excitement," Wexler said. "You don't get a lot of those opportunities. You might get a call or text in training to come out to play against the top guys, but I don't care what round it is: Just to see those guys is cool. But yea, I was kind of nervous. If you're going to do something worthy you're going to get nervous but I just remember gratitude. I was just super grateful. To be on that stage – just to make that stage – I don't even care who it was, to be honest. Just to make that stage was the cool part.

"It was satisfying and it was an honor, it was a straight up honor. And I remember going up to Todd Rogers before the match, shaking his hand and saying 'It's an honor just to share the court with you guys.'"

Wexler is a competitor, and he wants it known that, as a competitor, "I felt we actually had a chance to win. I did. I understand they were the number one team in the world or whatever but as a competitor, you gotta have that feeling – maybe not the whole time you're out there but at least for a little bit, right? I mean, 'Hey, maybe I can win!' I remember making this crazy dig and Travis runs way off the court, diving to set it, puts it up and it ends up being perfect and I put it down and we go crazy. After that play, I'm thinking 'Maybe we can win!'"

But he also knew, deep down, that those thoughts were largely delusional, that his odds were tantamount to Sisyphus finally rolling that boulder to the top of the hill. Dalhausser and Rogers had won five of the previous six AVP tournaments that season. They had lost just one match the entire year, in the semifinals in Atlanta a week before. Their next was not going to come at the hands of a team coming out of the qualifier.

So on the first point, Wexler couldn't help but laugh when Rogers "aces us on the most gnarly knuckle-ball floater I've ever seen. It started at Travis, went to me, back to Travis, we both crash into each other and they get an ace and we both start laughing like 'Alright, cool, here we are against the number one team in the world.' Looking back, yeah, man that was such a cool match to be a part of."

This is the first round of a main draw. This is how it goes. So you laugh. You make jokes. Because what else can you really do? Beat Thin Beast The Professor?

Think again.

Wexler and Schoonover lost, 21-10, 21-14. They lost their next match, too, falling to Mike Placek and Russ Marchewka, 21-13, 21-19. Just like that, their main draw experience was over. Two years of grinding and waiting tables and early mornings and late nights and couch surfing and fast food living… all for two blowout matches and $175 in winnings.

Congratulations, pro.

Wexler laughed about it. Because sometimes, when your reward to two years' worth of work is to play against the best team on the planet, on short rest, all you can do is laugh.

It is an experience that many a volleyball player has had, and almost all of them are the same, particularly the first-rounders. The match will be quick and painless. When a team makes it out of the qualifier and sees their names opposite Dalhausser, there should almost be a disclaimer on the bracket akin to the gates of Hell in Dante's Inferno: "Abandon all hope, ye who enter here."

In his decorated AVP career, through the 2016 season, Dalhausser is 47-3 in first-round matches against qualifying teams, and two of those losses, not surprisingly, occurred when he was hurt. Not that Dalhausser's uninterrupted dominance is a new phenomenon or breaking news. The abandoning of hope when facing Dalhausser began long, long before he ever stepped foot on the AVP Tour.

Dalhausser wasn't terribly similar to his athletic peers growing up in Daytona Beach, Florida. Sure, he was competitive, but if he wasn't good at a sport, he wasn't going to practice and practice and practice until he was. He'd just drop it on the spot. Forget it. Let's move on.

Basketball? Too physical. Golf? Terrible, and he hated how easy the professionals made it look. But volleyball? When his math teacher, who doubled as the Mainland High School volleyball coach, finally convinced him to give up baseball and come out for the volleyball team during Dalhausser's junior year, it came to him as naturally as tennis, which had been, up to that point, Dalhausser's favorite and best sport.

"The sports are really complementary," he said. "A [tennis] serve is almost the exact same technique as an arm swing in volleyball and the footwork is really similar so everything kind of came natural to me and I loved it right off the bat. I just became obsessed with it."

And Dalhausser was good, but still: This was boys volleyball – a "girls" sport, even in Daytona Beach. He went off to the University of Central Florida with aspirations to major in business administration and couple it with a graduate degree in pharmacy. Volleyball was "just kind of a hobby that I was obsessed with," he says. "I was probably down at the UCF courts more than I was at class."

Despite the long hours at the UCF sand courts and the short hours in the classroom, Dalhausser was like anybody else beginning to learn a sport: human. In the same way that Michael Jordan was famously cut from his junior varsity basketball team and John Elway tanked in his rookie season in the NFL, "nobody wanted to play with him," said Justin Phipps, who has been in and out of AVP main draws for more than a decade and lived in South Florida when Dalhausser made his debut.

"He would come out with this little defender and they might do some damage," Phipps continued. "But he didn't have it yet. But you knew it was only a matter of time."

Jody Pigford lived in Tampa while Dalhausser was making his ascent on the Florida circuit, small little cash tournaments under various "tour" names – Bud Light Tour, Toyota Tour, Florida Beach Volleyball Tour, Dig the Beach Series. During the first two seasons, Dalhausser was mortal. He would lose, sometimes even before the quarter- or semi-finals.

"At the beginning, it was just a matter of time before he would get it," said Pigford, who was raised in Tampa. "Everybody would say 'Man, as soon as this kid gets it, you know, there's going to be hell for all of us.' He was kind of sporadic, but he was still good. It was just like anybody else being a new player, he just happened to be so much taller and gifted than anybody else.

"It was just a matter of the ball control, the smart decisions, the right choices to make that would get you to those victories. It was like any new player, it was just a bigger scale. He jumped high and he was so tall, he was unbelievably raw and you really couldn't – he got it, but there's some players that have potential and if they keep doing it they'll be a decent player. But with him, it was 'He's going to be the best player in the world if he keeps picking it up.' The scale for him progressing and getting better was just totally different from everyone else because he had the tools everyone wanted or needed."

And so those first two years he lost – and he learned. Quickly. Those initial seasons are marked by limitless potential. The next two, after being picked up by a quicksilver fast defender from Davie, Florida named Nick Lucena, by uninterrupted dominance.

"They just made chump change out of us, pretty much," Pigford said, laughing. "Try not to get embarrassed is really what it was. It was just go in there and hustle as much as you can and they would make you feel like you need to reevaluate anything you thought about volleyball and 'Do I really want to play?' It showed you that huge gap where the rest of the volleyball players were and where they were. They just made lightweight use of us."

Well, they made lightweight use of those who actually stuck around for the tournament. Eventually, players, even the top-tier guys who could hang with Dalhausser and Lucena, began avoiding any tournament they entered.

"You would find out just from everybody playing around here down in South Florida, like 'Are Nick and Phil in town this weekend? Are they going to be there?'" Pigford said. "You always wanted to ask that question because for some of us it became where you were just throwing money away. We figured out if they were going to be in town or not, and if they were, some of us would pass. And it got that way with people who were really good. It's just not worth it to waste a hundred dollars to go get your butt smacked."

And those who didn't pass invariably did get their butt smacked.

"I always got the shit end of the stick," Phipps said. "I'd either play them in the first round or the second round every fucking time. You knew how it would go."

There remained, however, two teams who could beat Dalhausser and Lucena: An AVP-playing duo from Myrtle Beach named Adam Roberts and Matt Heath, and another from New Jersey. They would only come in town for the big tournaments, but when they did, they usually left with the money Dalhausser and Lucena had become accustomed to winning.

"Sure, man, they would lose some matches," Pigford said. "But you just knew that this was a different kind of athlete. This was a world class player. It was only a matter of time."

Imagine a 6-foot-9 beanpole of a man striping a road. That's what Dalhausser was doing when he got the call. Roberts, the defensive half of the team from South Carolina, had known Lucena and he had seen enough of Dalhausser: He wanted them to come live with him in his bachelor pad in Myrtle Beach. Imagine, his pitch went, if you trained with full time AVP pros, every single day, on their private court in South Carolina. Oh, and it would be rent free. Dalhausser practically put the construction hat down and started packing that day.

"He was thinking about taking a real job," Heath said, laughing at the thought of Dalhausser as possibly the world's largest pharmacist, which Dalhausser had planned on pursuing. "And we were like 'Hey man, let's try out this volleyball thing.'"

"I was like 'Huh, maybe I'll give this volleyball thing a shot,'" Dalhausser said. "They kind of showed us the ropes on the pro tour and it was a great situation for Nick and I."

It was an eclectic crew, to be sure. Growing up, Roberts had been an athlete who played seemingly everything *but* volleyball. He was raised in High Point, North Carolina on a steady diet of soccer, cross country, track and basketball, receiving offers from ACC schools to run the 800 meters but also an offer from Elon College, which was just 30 miles down the road, to play point guard on its basketball team. He took the full ride to Elon, started every game in his last three years and earned All Colonial Athletic Association honors. During breaks, however, he would live at his parents' house in South Carolina, and it was there that he discovered volleyball, a game that was quite similar to basketball in its movements – lots of quick, lateral steps and explosive leaps – but it was on a beach. So he would play pickup beach volleyball every day over the summers, and it paid off with an eight-inch increase in his vertical leap in the gap between his sophomore and junior years. In his junior season, he was leaping so high that he won a dunk contest.

"I had tried everything, man," he said. "I tried the strength shoes, the SuperCat Jump Machine. It wasn't until I began training on the sand with a weighted vest that I saw that increase, so I just used it as a cross-training sport."

And when he graduated with a dual-degree in business and econ, Roberts was good enough that he had some small-time offers to play basketball professionally in Europe. He wasn't interested.

"I was way too into volleyball," he said. So he spurned the offers overseas and moved to Myrtle Beach, where his parents had built a three-bedroom house on the beach.

"I said 'Sure I'll live for free on the ocean and play beach volley-ball,'" Roberts said, laughing. "It has a full hot tub, fire pit, a really nice volleyball court on the property on the ocean. It's a great set up and very conducive for guys to train in."

It didn't take long for word to spread of Roberts' volleyball pad in South Carolina. For nearly a decade, players cycled in and out, drinking and playing volleyball, living a life many dream of but few realize. And in the spring of 2003, when Roberts and his roommate, Heath, a 6-foot-6 former collegiate soccer player turned blocker from Fort Myers, Florida, were playing in a tournament in South Florida, they happened across "a skinny white kid and a tall guy wearing steel-toed boots" that were damn good.

"That," Roberts says, "is how I met Phil Dalhausser."

For almost two years, the four of them – Dalhausser, Lucena, Roberts, Heath – enjoyed the same, sublimely hedonistic routine.

"We would go out, I don't know, probably on average four times a week," Dalhausser said. "Adam pretty much ran the town so we'd drink for free. And those days we would roll out of bed at eleven or something like that and we'd stroll out to the courts at two."

After the hangovers had eased and they were able to play, they'd head out to the court and train for a few hours and then pore over film of Karch Kiraly and the greats at night.

"That house was volleyball one hundred percent of the time," Heath said. "We'd be on a road trip discussing 'Hey what do we do in this situation?' It was just kind of an open forum and we just did a lot of homework on it. It was a good time. We all raised our level."

But still, even in the Adam Roberts House of Volley, Dalhausser was different — "a freak," Heath said, and he means it as the highest of compliments. "His improvement was meteoric, to be honest."

When they popped in movies or played X-Box, Dalhausser would grab a volleyball and set to himself for all two hours.

"His concept was that he wanted really soft hands, almost that you couldn't hear it coming in and out," Roberts says. "That was his thing that he would set the ball so quietly that we could still watch the movie."

During the winters, Dalhausser and Lucena would pick up shifts as substitute teachers and Roberts would help out with Showstopper, his parents' dance competition production company. When it would be too cold to play on the beach, they took to the basketball courts, joining men's leagues and dominating pickup games. And it was there – not during passing drills or watching Dalhausser set to himself during movies or winning tournaments over the summer – that Roberts knew just how limitless Dalhausser's potential was.

"I had seen some good athletes, Division I basketball athletes, but when I saw Phil's touch on the basketball court – he could dribble, he had a good hook shot, he could bring the ball up the court – I was like 'Wow,'" Roberts said. "We played in a winter league, Nick is flying all over the court. I was like 'Man he is fast. Wow, these guys, especially Phil – their potential is limitless.'

"I had always equated beach volleyball with touch. You kinda have to shoot seventy percent as a basketball player from the free throw line to be a good beach volleyball player. The reasons being, I don't think Shaq could play beach volleyball because he couldn't set. But Phil had this touch. He's a different breed. Even to this day, being one of his best friends, knowing so much about him, I think you could do sports psychology just on Phil. He's just so laid back, so chill. You read these books and stories about Tiger Woods and Michael Jordan and their whole life goal was to win a gold medal and be a world champion and MVP, and that's not Phil."

As Pigford, Phipps, Roberts, Lucena, Heath and essentially everyone in South Florida knew it would, Dalhausser's reps began paying off. As a group, they would drive up and down the East Coast, playing whatever tournaments they could find. By the end of their third season in South Carolina, there was nothing left for Dalhausser and Lucena to conquer.

"The first year they moved up, we played them in the finals five times, and me and Matt probably won three or four," Roberts said.

"The next year was even, and the next, Phil and Nick won every single one of them."

"I had never seen anyone improve that fast," Heath says.

Everyone in the house knew: It was time. The West Coast was beckoning.

"It was the funnest two years of my life," Dalhausser says. "I had a blast. But we realized we weren't going to get any better."

Lucena went first, jetting off to Santa Barbara at the end of 2004, and Dalhausser shortly followed in the spring of 2005. Their decision was vindicated quickly, in the third AVP tournament of the season, when they took Austin, Texas by storm, beating the up-and-coming Jake Gibb and 2004 Olympian Stein Metzger 19-21, 21-16, 18-16 to win the tournament as the 10 seed.

In the decade-plus since, Dalhausser, through 2016, has won 83 tournaments on international and domestic tours. In that same time-span, he has lost just 64 total AVP matches, only four percent of which have come in the first round against a team out of the qualifier. And while only one qualifying team will have the misfortune of matching up with Dalhausser in the first round, it doesn't much matter: Either way, few rational people will expect you to win your first match. Or your second. Ryan Mariano knows.

In June of 2003, he thought he had finally "made it." For the first time in his career, he qualified on the AVP Tour, doing so with Jon Thompson. Even they were surprised.

"We were like 'Dude, seriously?'" Mariano recalled, laughing. "And then we proceeded to get throttled" by Eric Fonoimoana, a gold medalist in the 2000 Sydney Olympic Games, and Dax Holdren, a fifth-place finisher in the 2004 Athens Olympic Games.

"The problem is when you make it," Mariano continued. "Only then do you realize you're not fit to play on Tour. You get in, play a top-five seed, and you didn't realize you could get your tail beat that bad. I fell for every stupid trick in the book. It makes me cry trying to think about it. I fell for every single rookie trick in the book. It was oh, so fun. It was such an experience."

All told, Mariano would make a main draw by way of qualifier seven times. He didn't win a first-round match until his eighth main draw, in Manhattan Beach of 2004 with Ty Loomis.

"When you start making it into the top seeds in the qualifiers, and you qualify a little more, and you start to make the main draws, your mindset begins to change," Mariano said. "In your head, you have become a professional athlete. I loved that. And you get to party like a rock star and I loved all that stuff, too, and that was cool for a little while. But then you start looking at the next step. What do I have to do to beat him? And him?"

In April of 2005, Mariano partnered up with Heath in Austin, Texas, and came out of the qualifier and upset Canyon Ceman and Jason Lee in the first round. He would never have to qualify again. His reaction, in summary: Thank God.

"The thought of not making it once you've been there is terrifying," Mariano said. It is just a long and arduous journey to reach that point. But making it out of the qualifier and subsequently getting brutally humbled is a rite of passage in and of itself. It's something players take pride in, not much different from a battle scar from some grizzled veteran or a black eye from a fight. It's as if to say *Hey, I got in the ring and took my licks, and then I jumped right back in and did it again.* There's respect in that.

"So, you're a qualifier, play a top seed, maybe expect to give them a tough match," Dalhausser said. "Maybe not expect to win the match, but maybe make them sweat a little bit."

Because even Dalhausser, one of the most dominant athletes in American sport, lost four of his first five opening-round main draw matches.

"It's a tough road to try and get your first main draw win," said Billy Allen, who didn't even win a set in a first-round main draw match until his tenth main draw appearance. "It was a couple tournaments, my first couple qualifiers, I was just very happy to qualify and the expectation was almost – our work was done. We did what we came to do. And then your goals change to wanting to win your second-round match. Your first round is always going to be a top seeded team, but the second match is maybe doable. And then once you win that second round, you get some more points and you get better draws and instead of playing Phil in the first round, you're playing a team that's on par with you."

Added Hudson Bates, who retired in 2016 at the age of 31 after making an AVP main draw by way of qualifier seven times: "It's super tough, obviously, and I think that's what makes working all the way through that process all the more rewarding. I was proud I was able to accomplish that on my own. A lot of guys make it into main draw by partnering with a guy with a bunch of points, but that was never me. I was always left out because I live so far away [in Virginia Beach], and as hard as that was, I wouldn't trade it for the world because I can hang my hat on that."

One first round match in particular stands out to Bates. In late May of 2014, the AVP was hosting a tournament in St. Petersburg, Florida, and Bates and partner Mark Burik were the fifth seed in the qualifier. They cruised through their first two matches in straight sets, making it to the third and final round, where they would see Minnesotans Brian and Tim Bomgren. The heat index that day was north of 110 degrees and, as the 6-foot-5, muscle-bound Bates says, "my body type is not made to play volleyball in one hundred and ten degrees." But they survived, outlasting the Bomgrens 20-22, 21-15, 15-12. It was a seminal moment for Bates, though there was one not so minor issue: He had to wake up the next day and play the number two-seeded Tri Bourne and John Hyden.

"John is over there drinking his green juice, meditating, doing breathing exercises, barely warming up and not even sweating, and I'm in a full profuse sweat from the day before," Bates said, and he admits that he knew he had little to no chance of beating Hyden and Bourne simply from the fact that he had expended so much energy the day before.

True to his prediction, Bates and Burik didn't even last 40 minutes, losing 21-13, 21-14, which preceded a 21-18, 21-18 drubbing at the hands of Adam Roberts and Matt Prosser in the next round. It brings up an interesting balancing act for some of the top seeds in the qualifiers: Should they try to conserve energy in the qualifier, winning with as little effort as possible, so as to give themselves a chance in the main draw the next day?

Ask that question to Riley and Maddison McKibbin and you will get a resounding, unequivocal "hell no."

They would test that theory in San Francisco, the penultimate event of the 2016 season. The brothers had qualified in each of the past three events, accruing enough points to earn the third seed in the qualifier, meaning they wouldn't have to face a team seeded higher. On paper, nobody was better. In their previous two events, they had just barely lost in the opening round of the main draw, taking Ty Tramblie and Stafford Slick to three sets in Seattle and pushing John Mayer and Ryan Doherty to extra points in New York. Both matches, the McKibbins said, could have been decided by the fatigue from the previous day's qualifier. So, in San Francisco, they took their foot off the metaphorical pedal and, as Maddison says, "it blew up in our faces."

The first round was easy enough, a 21-13, 21-16 win that took all of 34 minutes. But the second round was markedly different. The McKibbins matched up with Cody Kessel and Dylan Maarek, two players who had been on the brink of breaking through for much of the previous two years but hadn't managed to put it all together. Kessel is, in the words of Maddison McKibbin, "a formidable fucking blocker" who plays indoor professionally overseas and hits the beach during the off-season. Maarek was one round away from qualifying in Manhattan

Beach just a year before and would eventually qualify twice in 2016. Simply put: It was the wrong team against which to conserve energy.

Which is why, later that afternoon, you could find the McKibbins with their father at a wine-tasting in San Francisco, drinking a little more than is likely recommended, stewing over a three-set loss and an early exit, the only tournament in 2016 in which they would fail to qualify.

"We were pretty fuckin' pissed," Maddison said. "We were pissed at each other. It was just – I don't even know. After that loss – that was really tough to stomach because we were capable of beating them but they played better than us. Luckily our dad was there, and we were gonna stay there until Sunday but we just went wine tasting. It takes a little bit of time to get over a loss, maybe some harsh words, but we get over it and it's onto the next thing. I can't stand that feeling. I don't like going back, really. It's just a tough thing to swallow. I think a lot of competitors are like that."

Added Riley: "It was an experience I'd rather not have, but it was a good experience for sure. Now we just say 'Alright, it's kamikaze time.' We would just always rather go down swinging and not put added pressure on ourselves. We don't need to qualify. Let's just play and have fun and see what happens."

Two tournaments later, they wouldn't have to worry about whether to conserve energy or not, whether to go kamikaze or not. They were, for the first time, automatically in the main draw at the final event of the season, in Chicago.

"We were elated," Maddison said. "We already had our flights booked so that we could practice before the qualifier, so we were there before any of the main draw teams. God, it was nice. It was really nice not to have to play in the qualifier. To end the season not having to play the main draw – that was our goal."

Without the added fatigue of the qualifier, the two cruised in the first round of main draw over Alejandro Parra and Gregg Weaver, 21-11,

21-12. Not coincidentally, it marked their first-ever opening-round win, and it ultimately led to their best finish (ninth) on the AVP Tour.

"That was our chance to come in strong, so we had such a sense of urgency to beat the first team we played," Riley said. "And we crushed them, because it was that level of just being thankful you didn't have to play in the qualifier."

As pitiless as the process is, and with the bitter taste of San Francisco still lingering, they wouldn't change a thing. And, for that matter, few on Tour would, either.

"It's brutal," said Trevor Crabb, who has only had to qualify four times in his already brilliant career on the AVP Tour and lost three of his opening-round matches succeeding the qualifier. "That's just kind of how you have to go about it – grind your way through the qualifier and play with whatever you have left on Friday. And you just keep doing it until you're in the main draw. If you get out of the qualifier every single time you're still not going do as well just because you had to play so much the day before. But I think it's good. It's a good thing to have to go through. It's a – what do you call it? It's a good rite of passage. You learn a lot, and you have to earn it."

In Huntington Beach in 2016, All four qualifying teams were dismissed as little more than inconveniences in the first round of the main draw. Not a single match even went three sets. Hell, not a single set finished closer than 21-15.

After Frishman and Brunsting were shooed away by Patterson and Gibb, they pulled out a three-set win in the contender's bracket over tenth-seeded Mark Burik and Hudson Bates before losing a thrilling three-setter to fifth-seeded Ty Tramblie and Brad Keenan. Meanwhile, fellow qualifiers Riley and Maddison McKibbin upset Casey Jennings and Billy Kolinske but bowed out the following round to Ryan Doherty and John Mayer. Avery Drost and Gregg Weaver went down in consecutive matches, failing to win a single set in the main draw.

But hope abounded amongst the qualifying teams in Miles Evans and Curt Toppel. Of all the qualifying teams, their path to the main draw was inarguably the most exhausting. Every single match went three sets, and no matter how well they played, they were going to match up with either Matt Olson and Kevin McColloch in the final round or Derek Olson and Jeremy Casebeer. Matt Olson had been one of the best players on Tour for more nearly a decade; McColloch had played in at least one main draw every year since 2008. Casebeer and Derek Olson were one of the most promising young duos on Tour, having just qualified for an FIVB Grand Slam in Rio de Janeiro a month prior, where they matched up with future gold medalists Alison Cerruti and Bruno Schmidt.

"Mentally, it's like 'What the hell?'" Matt Olson said. "I just saw those guys in Rio, now they're in the qualifier?"

But Matt Olson and McColloch upset the top-seeded Derek Olson and Casebeer, winning 21-17, 18-21, 15-10, meaning Evans and Toppel would have to go through them in the final round of the qualifier.

Miles Evans? Beat Matt Olson, an AVP winner?

Nah. Couldn't happen. Miles Evans wasn't good enough. He'd never been good enough. Even as a teenager at family reunions, he was never allowed to play in the volleyball games set up by his 10 aunts and uncles and dozens of cousins. They said he just wasn't good enough. He'd be a hindrance. Go eat some chips or something.

"I was like 'Fuck those guys,'" Evans recalled, laughing, though it's easy to hear the hint of residual anger that remains. That's the funny thing about teenage boys, though: They grow. And Evans sprouted up and up and up, past 6 feet, then 6-foot-1, then 6-foot-3, all the way to 6-foot-4.

Not good enough to play?

Joke's on you now.

To be clear, Evans still wasn't much good when he enrolled at Dos Pueblos High School. In fact, he uses the word "terrible" to describe just how bad he was. But it didn't matter. He was smitten, enamored with a game he only recently discovered was actually quite cool.

"I was terrible, I was hitting balls out, terrible," Evans said. "But I was athletic enough to make the team. That first year I really don't remember being successful but I just loved it, the fact that you could just hit the ball as hard as you possibly could at someone else, and let out just so much whatever is going on in my life – playing volleyball would get it all out."

Even on the days he was sick and had to miss school, he'd pop back in for volleyball class in sixth period.

"I was a gym rat," he said. "I loved the crap out of it."

And soon, unexpectedly, it loved him back. He joined a club team his senior year, and his swings caught the attention of the coaches at UC Santa Barbara, Cal State Northridge and the University of Hawaii. All of them extended offers for Evans to join their team. Not a single one of them realized that Evans wasn't eligible to attend.

He had never taken the SAT.

The thought that he might one day become good enough at volleyball to play in college had never occurred to Evans. He had worshipped the UC Santa Barbara team as a high schooler, watching his first collegiate match as a sophomore at Dos Pueblos.

"I'll ever forget that, dude, the guys were just studs, just bouncing balls," Evans recalled. "I was like 'This is what I want to do. I'm for sure doing this.'"

He just never took the steps to be eligible to do so. Out of necessity, he spurned the offers from UCSB, Northridge and Hawaii and instead shored up his academics at Santa Barbara City College. After two years in the junior college circuit, Evans was able to accept a scholarship to UCSB, and he shined, leading the team in kills and finishing second in blocks and aces. He was the go-to hitter on a strong team in the most volleyball-mad area in the country. It was only a matter of time before a professional team overseas extended a contract offer. Evans, though, wasn't sure that was what he wanted for his future. Perhaps it was a small stroke of serendipity, then, when Evans rolled his ankle prior to the start of playoffs during his senior season. He had to miss the post-season, the prime recruitment period for outgoing players seeking contracts overseas.

"I guess I wussed out," Evans said. "I didn't want to live by myself in another country. That idea scared the crap out of me."

Instead of taking a year-long contract to live in a foreign country by himself, he qualified, through USA Volleyball's developmental pipeline, for the Under 26 World University Games, which were being held in Portugal.

"That was eye-opening for me because I got to see all the guys my age in a different country and compare to where I'm at with them," Evans said. "It changed how I perceived beach volleyball, like 'Oh, people take this very, very seriously.' You can tell that these guys invested since they were kids. There are so many countries going five hours a day, double-days, five days a week, and I'm over here going for two hours and calling it a day. These guys are putting in work. It really takes a lot of hard work to get where they're at. That was a big eye opener for me."

For so long, Evans was devoid of a vision for volleyball. As a teenager, he only wanted to play in jungle ball games at barbeques. As a high schooler, he simply wanted to bounce balls. In college, he just wanted to play.

Then what?

After Portugal, Evans finally knew: He wanted to play professional beach volleyball. He had seen the AVP before, as a volunteer statistician in 2005 when the Tour stopped by Santa Barbara.

"I thought that was the coolest thing ever," he said. His first qualifier came in Huntington Beach in 2014, where he was throttled by Tim and Brian Bomgren in the final round, 21-16, 21-13. The next came a year later, in Chicago. Kevin McColloch and Matt Motter took him out in the third round, 21-14, 23-21.

But Huntington Beach of 2016 was different. Evans had a bona fide AVP-level partner in Toppel. They had won an AVP Next – a developmental tournament series for up-and-coming players on Tour – tournament earlier that year. Toppel had qualified for a main draw before. Evans knew this was his best chance.

"My expectations going in were that I was going to qualify, but deep down, I had this nervous, scared feeling, like 'I've never done it, I don't know if I can, I don't want to be embarrassed and lose this first match and look like a terrible volleyball player,'" he said. "All these things are going through my head before the first match and these guys just want to beat us more than anything and we're not playing that great, they're playing great, and we had to go to three.

"We had to come back in that first match and I had to step up and side out because I was getting every serve. I learned a lot in that match just what you can do late to earn points. When we won, it was just so much stress relief, like 'Wow we didn't lose first match I don't have to be embarrassed.'"

Evans and Toppel survived their first round, an 18-21, 21-8, 20-18 marathon against Chris McDonald and Danko Iordanov. Then they did the same in the second, edging out a 21-19, 22-24, 16-14 win over Daniel Dalanhese and Joe Hillman.

The third, against Matt Olson and McColloch, would be no different. Evans and Toppel won the first set, 21-17, and Evans had three swings for match point in the second, "but I flubbed them all out."

To three they went. And in that ninth set of the day, against all odds and self-doubt and fear of failure, Evans cobbled together enough plays to escape with a 15-12 victory, and his first main draw on the AVP Tour.

"That feeling – I was so fired up," Evans said. "So many people congratulated me. The reason why it felt great was that I was able to tell people I was a professional volleyball player for once, like I actually made it. Everything I'd been working towards – here I am."

AVP SEATTLE

*"I would never trade having a little bit nicer of
a car or a little bit nicer of a place for all of the
memories and adventures that we had."*

Where were Billy Allen and Theo Brunner?

They were just there, only two seconds ago! Everyone saw them! They had just crushed Avery Drost and Gregg Weaver in the semifinals of the AVP Seattle Open, 21-14, 21-16. It was a bit of a bore, really. But the finals, scheduled an hour later, promised to be a thriller, a matchup with the Crabb brothers, Taylor and Trevor, the hottest team in America. Allen hadn't played in a final in more than half a decade, when he and Brad Keenan lost to Sean Scott and John Hyden in a Jose Cuervo stop in 2011 in Manhattan Beach. Surely he couldn't just be...gone.

But he was.

Allen and Brunner skedaddled as soon as their semifinal ended, hopped in a rental van and high-tailed it to the Seattle-Tacoma International Airport. Two days later, you see, they were scheduled to play in an FIVB tournament in Hamburg, Germany. Allen had never played on the FIVB Tour, and he was predictably thrilled at the opportunity – but if he didn't check his bags, and checkthemrightthissecond, there was a good chance he'd miss his flight. Then again, if he checked his bags rightthatsecond, there was an equally good chance he'd miss the Seattle final.

To hell with it. They were going to make it work. Allen and Brunner zipped through the airport, checked their bags, raced back to the van, hopped on the highway, which was, of course, congested with a parade of red taillights. They both called the AVP, giving them updates on their status – *Ten minutes away! Five!* The AVP reserved a parking spot for them outside of the stadium. By the time they arrived, the women's final had already concluded, won by the young duo of Lane Carico and Summer Ross, and the Crabbs were lathered in sweat from warming up.

"We had no idea where they were," Trevor said.

"I was stressed out because of that, but it also helped out because it never gave me time to worry about playing in a final," Allen said. "We were just so worried about making it to the airport that it just kind of helped with the nerves."

Evidently so. Allen and Brunner beat the Crabbs, 21-19, 19-21, 15-12. You'd think he'd have taken a minute to celebrate his first win on the AVP Tour. Nope. Friends and family poured down from the stadium to congratulate him on his biggest achievement in more than a decade in professional volleyball, but he was already gone. He grabbed his wife, Janelle Ruen-Allen, an AVP player as well, and 6-month-old son, Ketch, and hopped back in the van with Brunner. It made for one hell of a crew: sweaty, stinking, beatific, stressed, overwhelmed, over-sized, infant, mother, aspiring international players who were also on the financial brink of needing another job.

Welcome to family life on the AVP Tour.

"Sometimes I think about if we both had real jobs, what the trade-off would be," Allen said. "And I would never trade having a little bit nicer of a car or a little bit nicer of a place for all of the memories and adventures that we had."

And oh, do volleyball couples embark on some adventures.

Beginning with that frenetic night in Seattle and ending with his flight back to the United States from Olsztyn, Poland, Allen, with his family in tow, would accomplish more in two weeks in terms of volleyball than he had in his entire career. He won an AVP tournament and then jetted off to Europe for his first shot at an international tournament. When his plane touched down at the Frankfurt Airport, United States beach coach, Rich Lambourne, a gold medalist on the 2008 United States indoor team, asked if Allen had ever been to that airport.

"And I said, 'Rich, I've never even been to Europe,'" Allen said, laughing. And then, with just one day to prepare for the qualifier in Hamburg, he and Brunner made it through, knocking out a soon-to-be Russian Olympic team of Dimitri Barsouk and Nikita Liamin in the final round. He'd beat another Olympic team, this one from Canada, in pool play and earn a shot against the viral, skyballing and jump-setting and street-balling Italian team of Adrian Carambula and Alex Ranghieri. Then he'd do it again in Poland the next week, qualifying and breaking pool, matching up with two more Olympic-bound teams.

"It was definitely happening so fast, like you weren't even taking it all in," Allen said. "It wasn't until on the way home from our FIVB trip that I was like, 'Oh yeah, that was pretty cool, I won that tournament.'"

And, oh yeah, I haven't been home in half a month.

Miami in 2007. That's where it started. Allen was playing with a 6-foot-4 blocker out of New Jersey named A.J. Mihalic. The duo had qualified for the final two events of the 2006 season, in Brooklyn and Boulder, Colorado. Allen was, strangely, for him, starting to feel like he belonged on Tour. And in Miami, the season-opening event for 2007, Allen and Mihalic qualified for the third straight time, winning their final two matches in the third set.

Allen's mind was elsewhere.

His eyes had been caught by a blonde named Janelle Ruen, who was playing with Jennifer Snyder and was automatically in the main draw after a successful 2006 season.

"Immediately I was like 'Who's this?'" Allen recalled. "Because she was really hot."

Allen was single. Ruen was single. The two would run into each other at AVP stops in Dallas, Huntington Beach, Glendale, Hermosa Beach and half a dozen more before the year was out. At some point along the lines, as Allen tells it, "she talked me into asking her on a date."

One date was all it took. Over the next few years, the two would travel around the country together competing, and "just being able to do that with somebody that you love is definitely special," Allen said. It's a common bond many beach volleyball players share. Casey Patterson met his wife, Lexi, playing volleyball at BYU. Nick Lucena, a 2016 Olympian, is married to current Florida State beach volleyball coach and former AVP star Brooke Niles. The two began as "workout partners," Lucena said, and "I couldn't stand her."

Lucena was actually dating Niles' partner at the time.

"When I think about it, it's crazy," he said. "I had no romantic feelings for her for the longest time. We just became really good friends, started traveling on the world tour and it just happened by accident. It completely changed my life for sure. I'm pretty fortunate."

Casey Jennings met his wife, three-time gold medalist Kerri Walsh, running wind sprints between lifeguard towers.

"I saw her from far away," he recalled. "I was doing sprints at a lifeguard stand, and I was doing sprints, and I saw someone walk up and start doing the same thing. I thought 'Oh, cool, someone's doing the same thing.' I was doing burpees and sprints, and afterwards I started walking towards the pier to my car and I see that it's Kerri. We started talking, and she asked me to a barbeque, and we went and hung out that night and the rest is history."

John Mayer, too, is married to a former Pepperdine Wave volleyball player and they now have an adorable young daughter and a little beach volleyball family.

"It's really cool that after matches I can ask her for her opinion and what she saw," Mayer said of his wife, who travels with him to every tournament, from Switzerland to Chicago to Austria to Manhattan Beach.

And if the wives of the players on Tour were never volleyball players, they are relentless and admirable and unequivocal supporters of their husbands' dreams. Just ask Jake Gibb.

★   ★   ★

Two years. That was the deal. Jane Gibb's 6-foot-7, 25-year-old husband, who had abruptly shifted his dreams from business to becoming a professional beach volleyball player, had two years, beginning with the 2003 season, to establish himself on the AVP Tour or the dream was over. She was pulling the plug. Time to get a real job and put the big boy pants on and go to an office and make enough money to support a family. Time to, more than likely, move back to Utah.

"For me it was hard," said Jane, who was born and raised in Utah and graduated from the University of Utah after spending two years at Dixie College in nearby St. George. "My whole family is in Utah, but I kind of thought we'd always go back. We were coming along so at the time it felt like an adventure. It was hard, and scary more than anything. It was more than anything in a million years I would have dreamed of. I did not imagine this life at all."

And there was, of course, the small problem that Jake had no idea what he was getting into.

"I had an unrealistic view of what the AVP was," Jake said. "I just kinda thought if you were a main draw player you'd be earning a living. If I knew the reality of it, I don't think I would have moved out."

Sometimes it's best to keep reality at bay. Ignorance, after all, is bliss. Had Jake done his due diligence, he would have known that the AVP had been in and out of multiple bankruptcies and had never really figured out a sustainable business model. He would have known that the top players were barely scratching out a meager living. He would have known that Eric Fonoimoana won four of the seven AVP tournaments in 2002, the season before the Gibbs moved from Utah to Southern California, and didn't even make $60,000. Jake was not yet a talent like Fonoimoana. He was not going to win four AVP events in his first full-time season. He was not going to make $60,000.

"It wasn't like I was moving out from Utah thinking 'I'm gonna be an Olympian, this is my road!'" Jake said.

"I didn't think he'd be a full-time professional volleyball player," Jane said. "I thought 'Ok we'll give this a few years and then he'll get a desk job. We'll have some fun before we have kids.' I never thought or imagined what actually happened."

What actually happened.

At first, not much. Jane took up a pair of jobs, getting into marketing while also putting her degree in exercise science from Utah to use as a personal trainer at 24-Hour Fitness. The marketing gig didn't last long, replaced instead by a job in mortgages, which Jane fell into when it was taking off in 2003.

So Jane would log 70- and 80-hour weeks. Jake went to the beach.

He found some success in that first season in 2003. Partnered with a loudmouth from Georgia named Ty Loomis, Gibb made it out of the qualifier in his first two events before dropping Loomis for Adam Jewell, with whom he would be seeded directly into the main draw. And still, even after making all eight main draws, even after snagging a fifth-place finish in Belmar, New Jersey, even after smoking Fonoimoana and soon-to-be Olympian Dax Holdren, Gibb made just $8,675.

"In the beginning, I was working a lot of hours for not a lot of money, so that was hard and I was like 'Please just do something,'" Jane says.

The next season, he did.

As it can sometimes go, it began with a stroke of providential dumb luck. One evening in the off-season of 2002, Jake and Jane, still new to town, were peppering in Laguna Beach. Little did Jake know, but Ryan Mariano, a full-time pro at the time, had biked down to the beach earlier that morning, and because he biked, he said he "wasn't going to stop playing until the sun went down."

Well Mariano saw "this tall, gangly guy over by the boardwalk, peppering with his wife" and asked him to play. Just like that, Gibb was in a training group with Mariano, Karch Kiraly, Larry Witt and Mike Lambert, a group that would combine for 140 wins on the AVP Tour (122 of them came from Kiraly alone). Mariano, though, was still playing professionally indoor overseas, and every summer he mulled over whether he should finally commit full-time to beach or continue to split his time between indoor and the beach. He figured once Gibb fully developed and harnessed his raw talent into something legitimately formidable, he'd hit the sand full-time, pick him up and they'd play together. But in 2004, Gibb's second season, Gibb didn't leave him much choice.

In the third event of the season, in Austin, Texas, as the No. 12 seed, Gibb and Jewell earned their first AVP victory, crushing Todd Rogers and Sean Scott in straight sets in the final, becoming the lowest-seeded team to win an AVP tournament.

"I saw that," Mariano recalled, "and I was like, 'Man, I'm never going to be able to play with this kid again.'"

The beach volleyball world had taken notice of Gibb. He finished out the 2004 season with Jewell, and was then picked up by Stein Metzger, who had just finished fifth in the 2004 Olympic Games in Athens. By the end of 2005, Gibb and Metzger were the No. 1 team on Tour, racking up four wins and making either the finals or semifinals in eight other tournaments. On the court, life couldn't have been better. Off of it, at home, there was inevitable tension.

"There was definitely some resentment because I was like 'You're traveling around the world and I'm stuck in an office every day,'" Jane said. "It was more that than anything. He was making fine money. It was more the resentment of 'You're going to go see the world and do something I would love to do if I was talented enough to do it.' So there was some kind of resentment, but yea I was so happy for him that he got to do such a cool job."

Jake did his best. Truly, he did. In 2005 and 2006, in an age before smartphones and Skype and FaceTime and Facebook and SnapChat, Jake and Metzger began traveling overseas. Each night, Jane would buy a calling card, and Jake would email her with the number and time to call him.

"It was just so much more difficult than it is now," Jane said. But they grinded and put in the incredible amount of effort it takes to make a marriage work, and soon, at the end of the 2005 season, in which Jake surpassed the six-figure threshold on the AVP Tour for the first time and supplemented it with another $48,375 internationally, there was no more calling cards and emails and grinding it out.

"That was the year that it was 'Oh, he's actually pretty good. He can support our family,'" Jane said. And that's exactly what he did. Jake was playing so well that Jane was able to get out of the office and didn't work an hour during the 2006, 2007 and 2008 seasons, in which Jake would make 22 AVP finals and cement himself as one of the top blockers in the world.

"It was kind of mind-blowing," Jane said. "Even the fact that he could attempt that was mind-blowing."

None of it was easy, of course. In 2011, when Jane was pregnant with their first child, the AVP was in the midst of yet another bankruptcy, meaning Jake had to head overseas for the season in order to make enough money to support the family.

"It was awful. It was terrible," Jake said. "We all want to play AVP and then supplement with FIVB. None of us want to play full time overseas. That was tough."

But he did what he had to do – which meant Skyping in from across the world to see Jane give birth to their son.

When Billy Allen and Janelle Ruen had their son, Ketch, Billy was at least in the hospital, but "we were way in over our heads," he said. "We didn't have any help."

They were both playing excellent volleyball at the time, which was great for the family income – but not so great when it came to watching and caring for their newborn child.

"I was literally handing him off to strangers while I was warming up," Billy said, laughing. "Luckily the volleyball community is pretty close, so I could be like 'Hey, Bomgrens, you look like nice guys, can you watch him for 10 minutes?'"

Finding someone to watch the kid while mommy and daddy go side out is likely the easiest part. Skyping and staying in touch – "We literally text all day long," Jane said – is inconvenient, sure, but modern technology is a miracle-worker for professional athletes. The really hard part?

How about this: There is no guaranteed money in beach volleyball. Unless you are one of the fortunate few talented and marketable enough to land a sponsor – in which case you likely make enough to be financially comfortable as it is – there are no contracts guaranteeing pay. No safety net should they tear an ACL or blow out a shoulder. With the sport being bereft of any semblance of a salary, there is an incredible pressure on a father or mother – or both – to win, and win and win and win, enough to support a family. It's a pressure that can be enough to force a player to retire without even giving it a shot. It's a pressure most humans choose not to handle.

Pressure for beach volleyball fathers is sitting on a 14-hour flight, crammed into the middle seat despite being 6-foot-6 with the limbs of a 6-foot-10 male. Pressure is dropping $10,000 on international travel with absolutely no guarantee of winning a single dime of it back. Pressure is heading into an FIVB qualifier, knowing that if one team gets to 21 points faster than you do in two sets, then that trip you just took to China? Over with. Money is gone. Trip's over. Savings are drained and oh, you've got a mortgage to pay and mouths to feed. Good luck.

It's a pressure Casey Patterson is frighteningly familiar with.

"That was scary," Patterson recalled of the summer of 2011, his first attempt at playing on the FIVB Tour, "because I went a whole summer on the World Tour and I barely broke even. I spent ten grand and I won ten grand. You do the AVP qualifiers and it's that [pressure] times a thousand. Because the only way you can make money is if you do really well. You have the whole flight to think about it, and it's like 14 hours, and you're in the middle seat. There's just so much noise in your head on those flights, you're like 'Oh my gosh, what's going to happen?'"

Spend five minutes with Patterson and one thing is unquestionably clear: He does not lack confidence. But confidence does not pay the bills. Wins do. And in 2011, Patterson wasn't winning. Not yet. And Lexi Patterson inevitably had questions.

"I had to keep convincing her that it was going to pay off in the long run," he said. "She was like 'What are we going to do? How are we going to stay alive?' I just kept saying 'I'm going to make it happen.'"

He was going to make it happen for no other reason than because he had to. And so he did what very few beach volleyball players have been able to do: He made it work, finding the precarious and tenuous balance between beach volleyball and a family. Patterson hustled. When he wasn't playing as an American duo with Brad Keenan, he was flying back and forth from Japan to play with Japanese legend, Koichi Nishimura. Patterson met Nishimura in Huntington Beach one day, when Nishimura was training in America. Though he spoke little to no English, Patterson didn't care. The guy could play ball. He didn't need a translator to see that. And Patterson needed somebody overseas to partner with and make a little extra cash. So Nishimura's sponsors would fly Patterson all over the world, from Japan to the U.S. or wherever in the world Patterson was playing that weekend – Norway, Switzerland,

Poland, Canada. Then they'd ship him back to Japan to run another tournament with Nishimura.

"I was ready to do anything, dude," Patterson said. "I just hit him up and was like, 'Where can I make some extra money?'"

Soon, Patterson found his answer. In 2012, after barely breaking even the previous year and in desperate need of money, he returned to the indoor scene, playing professionally for a year in Puerto Rico, commanding a salary he supplemented with the odd beach tournament with Nishimura that floated him to 2013, when the AVP returned with a seven-event season. And when he and Gibb began their sensational partnership in 2013, winning 10 AVP tournaments over the next three years while making more than $200,000 each on the FIVB, he was set. He had found how to make extra money: By putting in the miles few would, the repetitions most didn't, and living in a minimalist style many frown upon.

Most beach volleyball players, however, are not Casey Patterson.

Most, as J.D. Hamilton, a qualifier player from Mobile, Alabama, observed on the same day that Billy Allen and Theo Brunner were making their mad dash to the Seattle-Tacoma International Airport, are "just a bunch of crazy bums."

"Seriously," he said at the 2016 Laguna Beach Open, the biggest CBVA tournament of the year, "everybody out here is just a bunch of crazy bums."

The Laguna Open marked Hamilton's first trip to California. Over the past couple of years, Hamilton had made a name for himself as one of the best players in the southeast, an Alabama kid who was cleaning up the local cash tournaments. He made roughly $300 a week playing volleyball – winning a small, semi-competitive cash tournament somewhere within driving distance on Saturday and then another on Sunday at a beach volleyball complex called Tropics in Spanish Fort, Alabama. It didn't hurt that he was the only open level player within 50 miles of the place. He didn't care who he beat – he was making money, right? So beach volleyball became his method of paying rent and how he afforded his engagement ring when he proposed to his longtime girlfriend, Summer Bayles, at – where else? – a volleyball tournament in Fort Walton Beach, Florida. When told that the vast majority of beach volleyball players living in California, the mecca for the sport, lost no small amount of money in an attempt to make a living on the AVP Tour, Hamilton was stunned.

"So," he said, almost confused, "how do these guys make money?"

The short answer: most don't.

"I've had that pressure," Phil Dalhausser, a three-time Olympian and 2008 gold medalist, said, "where if I don't win this match, I don't eat."

That, of course, was many years ago, when Dalhausser and Nick Lucena – future millionaires both – were up-and-comers in South Florida. But it goes to show that it is a pressure that is near ubiquitous in professional volleyball, one that does not discriminate, whether you're a 20-something from Mobile or a three-time Olympian.

The most popular tours in California are the AVP and CBVA, which is arguably the best American tour not named the AVP. Most anyone who has ever had success on the AVP Tour has first risen through the ranks of the CBVA. There is, however, an inherent problem with the process: The CBVA doesn't pay. Not in any manner significant enough to call it an income. The winners of an open tournament might take home a couple hundred bucks each, with the exception of the Laguna Beach Open, which dishes out around $5,000-$10,000, depending on the sponsors. A few hundred dollars in winnings is hardly reason to jump into a volleyball tournament, particularly when considering the costs of traveling, tournament registration, Gatorades, snacks, parking – you basically only come out even. Not to mention time – the hours spent on the beach and in the weight room, training to win, well, what, exactly?

Pride and a check that might cover gas?

Hamilton was legitimately baffled by the economic black hole that is beach volleyball.

"Why do so many people live out here, just to struggle?" Hamilton asked aloud, not to anyone in particular.

He simply let the question hang out in the open, forever unanswered.

It's a question that inevitably sneaks into the mind of every volleyball player who has attempted to play the game professionally: What in the world am I doing?

"It's borderline irresponsible," Ed Ratledge said. "To be a full-time professional volleyball player is absolutely, borderline irresponsible. There are no contracts, so if you don't win or qualify, you don't make any money. If you get injured, there's no safety net. Unless you have a sponsor, you have to pay for travel, lodging, food and entry, which can add up to more than one thousand dollars. That means that you have to not only make the main draw, but probably finish fifth or better just to come out even."

It has been more than a decade since Ratledge has had to ponder his own volleyball existentialism. He had always, in his words, "been awesome" on a volleyball court, down to the first day he played on his church's volleyball court as a precocious preteen. That led to his joining a youth team in junior high, then the varsity team at Fountain Valley High School, then Long Beach State for three years before transferring to UCLA, where he won a national title, for two. And he is a fascinating specimen, Ratledge. He stands 6-foot-8, with arms so long that his fingers can scratch the bottoms of his knees when he walks. His hands engulf any they shake, and his massive feet are pigeon-toed, making for one of the most awkward gaits you've ever seen. But his lanky, limby build makes him a perfect blocker, either for indoor or the sand, and it didn't take long after his graduation from UCLA before he was offered a contract to play indoor in Portugal.

In 2001, Ratledge was sitting at a café in Portugal when he read about new rule changes to the beach game. The court would be cut down, from 30 feet by 60 feet to 26'3 by 52'6. The scoring had changed to the rally format we see today, meaning a point would be awarded on each play, no matter which team served.

"I'm thinking 'Boy, that really puts the onus on having a big block,'" Ratledge said. "So I got out, played the new rules, and qualified in Huntington, and we just smashed everybody in the qualifier. I was like 'Huh? I knew I was awesome but I didn't know I was this awesome.' I was 23, and I was an athlete, a little bit. I knew I was efficient with passing and setting but I was an indoor player. And if you're a good enough indoor player you can be a good beach player. I made that my mission."

His aspiration before his Huntington Beach epiphany had been an odd one, particularly for a 6-foot-8 mammoth of a man: Ed Ratledge wanted to be a pilot. He still does, actually, and has retained ambitions to fly commercially. That day in Huntington simply pushed his dream back a few decades.

Beach, though, in terms of a career trajectory, has nothing in common with indoor. Players competing on indoor clubs overseas can command six figure contracts. The best can even stretch it to seven figures. Guaranteed money. Paid lodging. Paid travel. The works. In beach, that's a laughable concept, a bad joke.

Six figures? Guaranteed? Haha!

Good one.

Yet oddly enough, it is the idea of going all in on yourself without much of a backup plan that has become the very heart and soul of the culture of beach volleyball, something that has been as much a part of the game as beaches and volleyballs and poles and nets.

"You're coaching or whatever your odd job is to pay for your beach volleyball hobby," Billy Allen said. "Then work gets in the way because you can't go to certain tournaments and you're coaching club and their season conflicts with your season and it's a tough balance. But if you want to be the best, you have to put volleyball first, and you basically have to be a bad employee on the other side."

When John Hyden, who played on the 1996 and 2000 United States Olympic indoor teams, was making his transition to the beach, he worked by installing Christmas lights and synthetic turf putting greens in San Diego. For six years, he worked a menagerie of such odd jobs until he began winning enough to live off of tournaments.

Imagine that: A two-time Olympian you watched represent your country, putting up your Christmas lights.

"It takes a lot," he said. "I'd train in the morning and I'd go to work all day. It's not easy but I knew I had to put the work in."

It is almost a rite of passage to sleep under a pier, or in a car, or on a couch too small, or a hotel room with four too many people in it – "we slept in the some of the gnarliest hotels," Patterson said – or, yes, even a bathroom stall, which is surprisingly more common than you might think.

But hey, we saved a couple bucks!

"You'd be surprised how comfortable a car can be," said Ben Vaught, a 21-year-old living in Huntington Beach who played in his first qualifier when he was 17. "I feel homeless sometimes, but whatever. No better sport in the world."

His English teacher at California Baptist University actually asked him one day if he was homeless. He thought she was joking. She wasn't.

On the surface, it does sound a little bum-like, hedonistic. Living on floors. Couch surfing. Sleeping in the trunk of an SUV. Using public showers. Owning so few possessions that you can fit all of them into a car with room for a passenger. Perhaps it's childish, an attempt to put blinders over the reality that unwittingly forces its way into our lives.

"I think there's a lot of escapism in beach volleyball," Ratledge said. "I think the movie Office Space spoke really loudly to my generation, just if you work in an office you're going to be miserable. All of my adult [players in the classes I teach] describe beach volleyball as the highlight of their week. I recognize every day just how lucky I am to live that life."

But still: It takes guts, and, as Ratledge says, "an unreasonably large sized ego" to pursue beach volleyball. "There's a reason a lot of beach volleyball players are gamblers. You have to be a gambler to do this. Betting on yourself is a good thing. I bet on myself a lot. I don't know if everybody's got the solid backing and the team behind them, the support system and the upbringing. How do you think I knew I was awesome? Because my parents are really solid people who are unconditionally loving who were my biggest backers always. I had the upbringing I needed to go out there and be confident in my awesomeness. Not everybody has that, but I really feel like that's necessary for people to chase their dreams. There's stubbornness, and betting on yourself."

It's just that betting that much on yourself, with a little percentage chance for a return, isn't for everyone.

★　★　★

John Moran was 7 years old when his father, at the behest of his older brother, Tim, hauled in 300 tons of sand and built a beach volleyball court in the backyard of their home in Phoenix, Arizona. Moran loved venturing out to the courts. The sand provided a sweet new setup to have imaginary GI Joe battles.

"I never played volleyball, which is really odd," Moran said. "Tim never let me play. But I got my feet in the sand and I'd bring all of my GI Joes out there and have massive sand battles and shit. But what it did do was expose me to the sand, and I just loved being in it."

Moran, like his three older brothers, was an athlete, but an average one. Good not great. He loved basketball but didn't have any offers to play at the Division I level, and the idea of going to a smaller school didn't really interest him. He wanted to go somewhere big, a place with a recognizable name.

A couple hours down the road, in Tucson, was the University of Arizona, with an enrollment north of 40,000. It fit the bill. And though it did not have a Division I men's volleyball team, for all intents and purposes, it may as well have. The club team – "the gold standard of club

volleyball," said Phil Dalhausser, a former club player at the University
of Central Florida – offered six full ride scholarships and two partials.
With a coaching staff who recruited players as any other Division I
team would, Arizona was one of the best club teams in the country, a
perennial power that could compete at the Division I level – and proved
it could in regular scrimmages with UCLA – had it been sanctioned
by the NCAA. While other club teams would bus to tournaments,
Arizona would fly.

"It was crazy, and we were just paying 25 bucks a month in club
dues," Moran said. "I've talked to a lot of guys who have played club
volleyball and apparently my experience was very different from theirs."

Despite starting for a glitzy club team, Moran knew there was no
professional future for him in regards to volleyball. Teams from Italy
and Switzerland and Portugal were not calling to offer him contracts –
but the Arizona State Legislature was. It offered him an internship,
which he parlayed into a full-time offer. It was a no brainer.

He turned it down.

He hated the job, hated the politics, got out.

Conveniently, a buddy of his, Geoff Pollard, called Moran out of
the blue and told him he was moving to California. Would he like to
come? Moran figured what the hell. He already spurned the job offer
he had just spent the last four years studying to earn.

What did he really have to lose?

"I just moved out with him on a whim, because isn't that what
everyone does? Turn down a career and move to California? That's just
my personality," Moran said. "I'm not very analytical. I'm a doer. I was
just like 'Yep, this makes sense. I'm going to do it.'"

Moran liked volleyball, and he was still intent on playing it. But
he also liked financial stability, which couldn't have been farther down
the economic spectrum from professional volleyball. And his decision
to keep his job higher on his hierarchy of needs than volleyball can be
boiled down to two of what he refers to as "aha moments."

At the time Moran moved to California, in 1998, a man named Jon Moleski lived in a house on the 22nd Strand in Hermosa Beach. It had a pool, was an objectively beautiful home, in one of the most desirable locations in the United States. He was also the interviewer for Moran's first job as an executive recruiter when Moran made his move.

"You see this house? You see my car? You see this life I have?" Moleski said. "Listen, I moved here from somewhere else too and I played volleyball, but you can't get what I have playing volleyball."

Moran nodded, ruefully, the sad reality beginning to dawn on him.

"I just made a decision right then and there, and I don't know if maybe I would have reached my full potential if I would have been playing volleyball full-time but I always knew my career was more important, finances always had to be in line," he said. "Volleyball was a passion of mine and I wanted to play on the AVP but I didn't want to sacrifice my career."

He didn't.

As an entrepreneur, Moran achieved a level of wealth that would make his old interviewer blush. Which is exactly what led to his second "aha moment" nearly 10 years later.

A financially savvy individual, Moran likes to keep a spreadsheet detailing his expenses and revenues, which makes him a fairly normal adult male – and something of a unicorn on the AVP Tour

"I've literally never seen another guy keep a spreadsheet," Moran said, incredulously. "I treat it like a business."

And in 2009, his spreadsheet was thicker than it had ever been. Back-to-back ninth place finishes on the AVP Tour netted him nearly $4,000. A string of four consecutive thirteenths left him with close to another four grand. All told, he would make main draw in all 13 AVP events that season. He would win CBVA tournaments and a massive cash tournament in Seaside, Oregon, which draws as many fans as AVPs.

And after all that, after his best year as a professional beach volleyball player, Moran made hardly a little more than $16,000.

It was less than a quarter of what he sometimes made in a month.

"That was a lot of work, and I made sixteen grand!" he said. "How could you ever make that – and I get following the dream – but how could you ever make that your number one priority? When I got to the end of the year I was like 'Holy shit! That was a lot of work for sixteen grand!'"

What's worse is that most beach volleyball players would kill for 16 grand. In 2016, 79 players were issued a paycheck from the AVP Tour.

Only 10 made more than $16,000.

"I had a month where I was making $72,000 [as an entrepreneur]," Moran says. "That was a single month. I remember getting that check in my bank account and turning around and looking at the AVP Tour and not one dude, not one dude on the AVP made what I made in a month, playing an entire year. There wasn't a dude who made seventy-two grand playing the whole fucking season. That was an 'aha moment.'"

Seventy-two grand? As a volleyball player? In 2016, Patterson and Gibb, who finished the season ranked No. 1 and 2 on the AVP Tour, didn't even *combine* for that sum.

"I've made, like, $100,000 in the past four years on the AVP Tour," said Nick Lucena, a 2016 Olympian who made 10 AVP finals from 2013-2016. "It's a joke."

So no, the aha moments are not limited to Moran. Far from it. The lightbulb will eventually flicker on for every player who can't make main draws on the international tour, where there is enough money to provide a steady income. Even players like Kevin McColloch, a 32-year-old from Solano Beach who made history at the AVP's stop in Seattle in 2016 by becoming the first 16 seed to beat a 1 seed in an AVP main draw, have learned, for better or worse, that volleyball is not a sustainable career.

Sometimes it just takes a little longer for the lesson to sink in.

"From when I was about sixteen to twenty-five, I don't think anybody – well, Ty Tramblie plays a lot of volleyball – but I don't know if anybody put in more hours than I did," McColloch said.

He earned a scholarship to Holy Names University, a tiny school in Oakland with an enrollment of less than 1,500. McColloch didn't really mind the lack of name recognition. Holy Names offered an opportunity for him to play ball with a free education on the side.

"Money was an issue," he said, "so that was big for me."

He'd practice for three hours on the beach before heading over to practice with the Hawks indoor team, showing no signs of burnout or fatigue.

"I would just play all the time," he said. "I would play every tournament. I was just constantly, constantly playing. I never had any technical teaching. We'd just roll out balls and come up with drills."

It paid off in the form of an overseas contract, in Belgium, where after just a handful of years' experience he had been signed as a professional volleyball player.

"I didn't have the best experience over there," he admitted. "It was fun, like I was a professional, getting paid and stuff. But I got homesick, and it was snowy so I never really got to play beach. So I kind of had to decide: beach or indoor? I decided to go all in with beach."

By all accounts, he has had a successful career, cashing out in 44 professional beach tournaments through 2016, becoming a mainstay in the AVP's main draw. Even still, he knows: "I don't think it's possible for me, just with money and everything, to only be a professional volleyball player."

In July of 2014, he married fellow professional beach volleyball player Ali Daley. In the fall of 2016, they were discussing starting a family. In McColloch's entire career, which spanned more than 10 years, he had made less than $45,000 in sanctioned professional events. He understands numbers, and he especially understands them when they don't add up.

"Who had a good year this year?" he asked, rhetorically, referencing the 2016 season. "Let's go with Billy Allen. The guy won a tournament this year, right? Had a great year. He made twenty-two thousand bucks, you know? That's peanuts. He's ranked sixth in the country, and he made twenty-two thousand. And this is Southern California. It's not cheap to live here."

Indeed. Housing alone is 157 percent higher than the national average. For one adult in Southern California, the annual income needed to cover basic household expenses is estimated to be just a hair below $30,000, and that does not factor in the expenses of traveling around the country to play volleyball. It's fair, then, to ask the question with no simple answer: Why invest so much time and effort in a game that, at the end of the day, does no favors to the bottom line?

In 2016, Raffe Paulis, a professional who has been in and out of main draws since 2009, helped McColloch find his answer. The two were training in Manhattan Beach, and McColloch was having an uncharacteristically rough day. He would miss a high line, shank a pass, botch a set. And then he'd throw his hat. Slam the net. Sulk. They retreated to Paulis' apartment afterwards to take a look at the film. McColloch was startled by what he saw.

"Raffe said 'Dude, look at your body language. You're miserable. You're not having fun. Why are you even playing?'" McColloch recalled. "I don't think Raffe thought anything of it, but I thought about that for a week. Having fun is just so much more important to me. I'm playing better when I'm lighthearted and smiling and interacting with the crowd.

"I never wanted to make a career out of beach volleyball. I didn't want to move to [Los Angeles]. I didn't want to put all the work in that Casey [Patterson] and Jake [Gibb] do. That's their life, and I have a ton of respect for them, but that wasn't me.

"It just fulfills your brain wanting to fill out a strategy. You train and you feel good the rest of the day. It's just fun to do. I love practicing and training because it just makes my day better. I think you just have to pick and choose your battles. I didn't play New York because I didn't want to, you know? I didn't want to fly across the country, pay three hundred bucks for a hotel. I've seen New York. I don't think it's that great. So I didn't play.

"Me and Ali both wanted to pursue it, and we both cared enough to play. We had a balance, and last year she paid for a coach and training, and I supported that one hundred percent. I want her to do it until she doesn't want to do it anymore. Now we're talking about having a kid, she's working hard as a paralegal, doing a lot of other things. We didn't want to get to a point where we're both forty years old, our bodies can't do it anymore, and we're like 'What do we do now?' Volleyball is not everything for us anymore."

But it will always be something, a concept in which many players can relate. For some, volleyball is the very bedrock upon which their lives are built.

That's how it has been with Allen. His victory at Seattle was a long, long time in the making. He cannot recall a single weekend in his childhood that he and his family did not trek down to Oceanside to play beach volleyball and barbeque all day. His parents had met playing the game, though only recreationally. Much of Allen's childhood revolved around the game, whether playing it himself as a 10-year-old in his first grass tournament or tagging along to his parents' matches. Eventually, inevitably, Allen grew passionate enough that he wanted to join a club team, though instead of simply signing his son up, Bill Allen made his own team. Serving as their uniforms were six pairs of matching shorts that Bill had bought from Ross.

It was low level, sure, but it was good enough to prepare him for high school, where he became the team's setter, and he proved that he could set well enough to earn a spot on the team at Cal State Northridge. He would practice with the team and then he and Ty Tramblie, his roommate with whom he battled – "and mostly lost," Allen said, laughing – for the starting setter position would head out to the beach and play. And even when Allen and Tramblie began winning high level CBVA tournaments, he didn't think much of it.

"I never thought volleyball was realistic," said Allen, who has an endearing habit of overwhelming self-deprecation. "I was never that great of a player. I was never in the mix indoor as far as being an All-American who was going to go overseas and make a bunch of money."

But after graduation, in that enviable period between school and a job some refer to as a "gap year," Allen and Tramblie, neither of whom stand a millimeter above 6-foot-2, signed up for the AVP Huntington Beach Open – and qualified.

"We split-blocked [where the players rotate as blockers, rather than one being the blocker and one being the defender] back then, which I know is funny to think about," Allen said. "We would just jump serve as hard as we can and split block. We didn't think twice about it. Ty would be up there trying to block [Mike] Lambert."

Despite his astonishingly quick success, Allen never saw volleyball as anything more than a hobby. He had majored in communications and landed a job as a page with Paramount Pictures, an auspicious start to a career he fancied might take him to video production. Volleyball was, at best, an afterthought, and he wouldn't play a single professional tournament in 2005.

"It was so expensive just traveling to New York and Florida. I thought it was crazy to spend all that money on airfare and hotels and stuff," he said. "I got a little taste of it, and maybe I wasn't confident enough."

Volleyball circles in California, however, run small. And when Allen joined a casual game of four-on-four in Santa Monica, a man named Jon Mesko couldn't help but notice that Allen had a gift for the game.

"The guy was just awesome to watch and play, and he just kept digging me, and I was like 'Who is this guy?'" recalled Mesko, who had played in 11 AVP qualifiers by that point but hadn't yet made a main draw. "Sorrento is an old-school beach and he worked well with all the attitudes and that's an impressive characteristic."

In their second AVP qualifier together, in Huntington Beach, the two made main draw.

"I remember that like it was yesterday," Mesko said, 10 years after the fact. "It was gnarly. We had been working hard, training with [Brad] Keenan and [John] Mayer, training with some tough teams. We had to play in the first round and we had to play this team that was medium hard, we handled them about eight a.m.

"Then we play the four seed in the second round, Dave Fischer and Scott Hill, and they were kind of the big boys. They were the team to beat in that bracket and they were probably favored at that point, like five to one or ten to one, and we just came out and absolutely ripped jump serves and caught them by surprise and they just didn't really see it coming. We shocked them. But you beat the four seed in your bracket and you think it's over, but it was far from over.

"We had to beat Reuben Danley and [Shigetomo Sakugawa] next, which was a good team, they were tough. Reuben rips jump serves and Tomo digs everything so we beat them and we're sitting there and it's three or four in the afternoon, three tough matches and we still have another one, and it's Kevin Dake and Jeremie Holmes. The end of the day, that's where conditioning comes into play, and Jeremie Holmes is cramping and struggling and we ended up beating them as well."

Going from seeded Q60 to main draw was enough: Billy Allen was getting back in the game.

"Once I got on the road and made it happen, made that commitment, that's when it became more realistic," he said. "And again, I made my goals pretty small, pretty attainable, and so it was if I broke even that would be awesome. It's crazy at this point to be where I am now, being permanently main draw and winning a tournament. I never thought that was going to happen when I got out of college."

Yet it did. And in the dozen and counting years that followed, Allen would win an AVP tournament and become one of the top defenders in the country. It's all still crazy to Allen, that he's able to tell people he plays volleyball on a beach for a living, that sponsors pay him money to wear their logos and gear, that he met his wife and started a family around a sport in which he saw no future.

Stories like Allen's are what motivate many to keep going, to keep pushing, because who knows? Maybe they can make it all work too. Maybe they won't have to balance work and volleyball. Maybe, one day, they won't have to make a distinction between the two.

Maybe they can make this beach dream work.

AVP NEW YORK

"It was a moment to celebrate."

Amy Grabiec had never been to New York. An Arizona native, she had only flipped through pictures. She wanted to see that iconic skyline, wanted to view the sprawling city from atop the Empire State Building, wanted to marvel at Times Square. Basically, she wanted to be a tourist.

She just didn't want to become one so fast.

Sure, Grabiec wanted to see the city and all, but on June 16, 2016, before the sightseeing, she wanted to qualify for the AVP Tour, which was playing its fourth tournament of the season in the Big Apple. She had flown in to play the qualifier with a talented partner, an All-American from USC named Lauren Sieckmann. They were scrappy, with tremendous ball control and crafty shots.

They had no chance.

Grabiec knew it. Sieckmann knew it. Everyone who saw the bracket knew it. For on their portion of the bracket were two names that nobody – not a qualifying team, not even a main draw team – would have wanted to see.

In the second round, barring a monumental upset, they'd have to play Sara Hughes and Kelly Claes.

The future of beach volleyball is exactly what you might imagine: blonde hair, blue eyes, sunkissed skin, smile straight out of a toothpaste commercial. Laid back, easygoing, amiable. A marketer's dream.

And a girl.

There are certain athletes who are so gifted that it almost seems unnatural, otherworldly, unfair. In sports, there's a term for that: God-gifted. Karch Kiraly was one. Tiger Woods was one. Michael Phelps was one. Michael Jordan? Nope. Not even No. 23 can fall into this category, for he was famously cut from his high school team.

Sara Hughes has never been cut from anything.

Lauren Hughes is the eldest of Rory and Laura Hughes's children. She was a gifted volleyball player herself, a three-time captain at Mater Dei High School, an athletic powerhouse in Santa Ana, California that has produced the likes of NFL quarterbacks Matt Barkley and Matt Leinart, who is perhaps the best quarterback in USC history. Lauren Hughes was their peer, a three-time MVP who led the Monarchs to a Trinity League title in 2006.

But who was that little blondie tagging along to every tournament, begging her mom, Laura, to just please please please pepper with me? She passed everything perfect, set well, hit everything right onto Laura's platform. It didn't go unnoticed. At one of the countless tournaments that Sara was hauled to watched her sister, Lauren, and brother, Connor, play, a parent approached Laura, slightly stunned at the precociousness of this little girl she was peppering with.

"I know someone I'd love to introduce you to," she said, and Laura told her that she'd be happy to take his call.

His name was Bill Lovelace – Pajama Bill, as he was affectionately nicknamed, for his proclivity of showing up to the beach or gym in pajamas, a long sleeve t-shirt, and enough zinc to block the sun even if he moved there. Raised in Long Beach, Lovelace played for Long Beach State, and after graduating with a degree in Physical Education, he joined the Coast Guard, taught PE on the side, and voluntarily coached anyone willing on the side of that. It didn't take long for news to spread of the former player giving out coaching lessons to dozens of players, free of charge. Kids and parents flocked to his court in Huntington Beach for free lessons and tryouts.

So when Lovelace called Laura Hughes in 2003 and offered to coach her youngest and wildly talented daughter for free, who was Laura to turn him down? A few days later, 8-year-old Sara and childhood friend Matt Butler met Lovelace for a tryout in Huntington Beach. When Laura came to scoop Sara up a few hours later, she asked Lovelace how her girl did.

"She has the best ball control I've ever seen for someone her age," he said. "She should come down and train on Tuesday and Thursdays for free, and I already have a partner for her."

Two days of training per week? From a coach? For free? With a partner?

Deal.

So it was that every Tuesday and Thursday, Sara, Matt, and her partner, Justine Wong-Orantes, would head down to Huntington Beach and practice with Lovelace.

"That's when I knew, that first tryout I had, I was at the beach, I had a volleyball in my hand, and I was like 'This is what I want to do. This is a dream come true for me,'" Sara said. "I would just be at the beach from eight to five, playing with my friends, playing and then going to the water and getting food and then going back down and playing some more. So I'd just be down there all day and my parents would just pick me up hours later. It was amazing."

It was perfect timing. Just a few courts down were Misty May and Kerri Walsh, Olympians both who were quickly rising up the ranks on the FIVB. They were considered likely to win a gold medal after a year on the AVP Tour in which they went 39-0 and won all eight tournaments. It was the first time anybody had gone undefeated on a beach volleyball tour of any kind. Internationally, they won five of eight tournaments, reaching at least the semifinals in every single one.

When her practices would finish, Sara would plop herself on the wall in Huntington Beach and watch May and Walsh, studying their movements, watching them compete, dreaming of becoming them.

Fifteen years later, little girls now dream of becoming Sara Hughes. In her first full season as a professional, in 2017, a parent would pull her aside, tell her that her daughter had a poster of Hughes hanging on her wall, that she has aspirations to become the next Sara.

"I was like 'No way is that actually happening,'" Hughes said, laughing. It was just as Lovelace had predicted about that little blondie with the unbelievable ball control. If Lauren had been good at Mater Dei, Sara was a phenomenon. In 2009, her freshman year, Sara was named the team's best defensive player, and she matched her sister's MVP count by taking the honors the next three seasons. She became All-League, then All-America. The Orange County Register dubbed her the Player of the Year. The school named her the Female Athlete of the Year as a senior. Her GPA finished at 4.0. She was every parents' dream child and, in high school, a college's fantasy: divinely talented, humble as can be, likeable, smart, hard-working. Virtually every school on the West Coast called and sent letters: Stanford, UCLA, Pepperdine, Hawaii, Arizona, Long Beach State, Washington, San Diego, Loyola Marymount, UCI, Berkeley. Florida and Texas and North Carolina threw their names in the hat as well.

Hughes had two requirements. The first was that the school had to be located in California. Sorry, Florida, Texas, and UNC. You're out. The next was that it had to have a beach program, which the NCAA recognized in August of 2010, Sara's sophomore year at Mater Dei, as an "emerging sport," meaning it wasn't quite sanctioned by the NCAA, but was well on its way. The NCAA required 40 schools to sponsor a beach team, a number it hit within just five years, creating a welcome trickle-down effect as well: Division II and III schools were also adding beach programs, making beach the fastest growing sport in NCAA history.

"It was a moment to celebrate," said Marilyn Moniz-Kaho'ohanohano, the NCAA Beach Volleyball Committee's chair and associate athletics director at the University of Hawaii. "This is an opportunity to give girls a chance to dream about being able to get a scholarship, to go to college. For the more elite and dedicated player, it could be a step into becoming a professional beach volleyball player and playing in the Olympics."

The Olympics. That had been Hughes' goal all along, since those days as an 8-year-old sitting on the Huntington Beach wall watching May and Walsh, living representations of her dreams.

She loved indoor, truly. And she loved being recruited – everybody was so nice! But she had to make a decision. As hard as it may have seemed – indoor or beach? UCLA or Stanford? San Diego or UCI? What about Berkeley? – it was actually rather simple.

USC had been hard on the Hughes recruiting trail, but the Trojans already had three setters. It also had a beach program. It also resided in California, just a 45-minute drive from Hughes' home in Costa Mesa. It also had Anna Collier, the head coach of the beach program who had been a professional player herself and once coached May and Walsh.

Ding ding.

Hughes took one visit to USC and The Great Recruiting Chase was over. The facilities! The stadium, which was just for beach volleyball! Coach Anna!

She was a USC Trojan. She didn't tell anyone.

"I didn't want to hurt people's feelings," she said.

The best volleyball player in the country, the one with the three MVP awards and offers from nearly every school in the country, the one with a perfect GPA, didn't want to hurt people's feelings.

A dream.

Her college career quickly became one.

In her freshman season, Hughes teamed up with 6-foot-2 blocker

Kirby Burnham, a senior who had been recruited out of nearby Newport Harbor High School, and they set a USC single-season record with 42 wins and a national championship. For Burnham, it marked the perfect send-off to a decorated USC career. She won two national titles and in 2013 became the beach program's first-ever All-American. One might think that losing an All-American, two-time national champion partner might portend a down-season for Hughes. One might also think wrong. When Burnham walked across the stage and tossed her cap into the air and called it a career, in her stead stepped Kelly Claes.

A new era of USC beach volleyball was born.

★ ★ ★

"Is the red-head yours?"

Craig Tefertiller had to find out who the tall seventh-grader with the reddish orange ponytail was, swatting shots, hammering swings, setting dimes. She was exceptionally tall, even for a volleyball player, and yet she didn't possess any of the awkwardness one might expect from a girl who grew earlier and taller than the rest of her peers. His search for her parents may not have been the most scientific, but it proved prescient: Find the tallest guy in the stands. Standing 6-foot-7, Paul Claes, a former baseball player at San Diego State, was tough to miss. Tefertiller sat down next to him, asked him if that red-head dominating the middle was his.

"Yup. She's mine."

Tefertiller gave Paul the rundown: He was a volleyball coach for Impact Volleyball Club in nearby Yorba Linda. He ran camps and also coached the U-14 club team. He'd love to have Kelly come out for a practice. Kelly certainly wasn't opposed. She loved basketball and softball and track, but volleyball was pretty fun, too. Why not? To Tefertiller's camp she went, and she discovered that volleyball came more naturally to her than anything else. She used her approach for layups to run slides, an offensive play in volleyball in which a hitter takes off of one foot rather than two, which is, conveniently enough, the exact footwork used when shooting a layup or driving to the hoop in basketball. Her footwork for fielding a ground ball in softball was exactly that of passing a volleyball. Her throwing motion mirrored that of a volleyball swing.

"I would call it a little unconventional," she said, "but it worked for me, so I had a great time doing it."

It also worked out that Tefertiller was the longtime coach at El Dorado High School, a volleyball powerhouse in Placentia, just a short drive from Claes' house in Fullerton. Claes was the cornerstone of another successful four-year run for El Dorado, which won 19 league titles in Tefertiller's first 20 years, and the college coaches, just as they did with Hughes, came calling.

Her commitment process wasn't much like Hughes'. Claes loved Long Beach State. Long Beach State loved Claes. She offered the 49ers a verbal commitment when she was a sophomore and then continued dominating the high school scene. The coaches at Long Beach, which was scheduled to have a beach program by the time Claes enrolled, encouraged her to try the sand, just to see.

"Go try it," they said. "Have fun. It's no big deal."

They had no idea they had just given away their prized recruit.

In the same way that Bill Lovelace knew immediately that Sara Hughes was going to be an incredible talent, he had that same feeling with Claes. Tall, coordinated, well-mannered, passionate. Possessing both the tangibles and intangibles. Can't beat it. So Claes would run through drills with Lovelace, and while she liked the beach, she didn't become attached. Indoor was still her game.

Until John Aharoni got ahold of her.

"Who the hell are you and where did you come from?"

Those were the first words Aharoni spoke to Kelly Claes, at a try-out for the USA Volleyball High Performance U-19 team. It was the summer between Claes' junior and senior seasons at El Dorado, and she had been seeking any avenue of volleyball competition, and no program featured a higher level of competition or quality coaching than USA Volleyball's High Performance beach team.

"I'm from forty-five minutes inland," Claes said. "I've just been playing indoor."

Not anymore.

She made Aharoni's U-19 beach team, which also featured a 5-foot-10 blonde by the name of Sara Hughes.

"I didn't know what type of caliber player she was," Claes said. "I mean, she had been playing on the beach since she was eight. She had traveled a lot before, so honestly when this little blonde girl came up to me and said 'Hey! Do you want to play together this summer?' I was like 'Well we practiced well together and you seem like you're pretty good so sure, I'd love to play with you!'"

Quiet thunder had just struck.

At the end of the summer, Hughes and Claes traveled to Portugal for the U-19 World Championships. This was nothing new to Hughes. She had already competed in Croatia and Canada, Thailand and Cyprus. It was the first time Claes had ever left the country.

"I never dreamed that my sport would take me to such amazing places," Claes said. "Growing up, it didn't seem like a realistic idea."

Before she left, Aharoni and USA Volleyball coach Barbra Fontana told Claes that her vision for her future was about to take a dramatic shift.

"You're not going to play indoor anymore after this," Aharoni told her. "After you go, and you're sitting there on center court, and you look around and see the crowd, and you look at where you are in the world, you are not going back to indoor. You're going to realize how much you hate being in a gym."

"Ooookkk, John," Claes responded, not believing a word.

And then she had that exact moment Aharoni spoke of. Hughes and Claes won their first two matches, clobbering a team from Niger 21-0,

21-3. They kept it going all the way to the semifinals before losing to a Brazilian team that, four years later, would just fall short of qualifying for the 2016 Olympics. No matter. They rebounded and won the bronze medal match in a thrilling three-setter over Germany. And wouldn't you know it, they did it on a packed stadium court. Claes knew right then, playing for that bronze medal in Porto, Portugal, that she was not going to play indoor in college, just as Aharoni told her she wouldn't. While she had been verbally committed to Long Beach State for nearly two years, nothing had been signed. She was still an open recruit, and the two most important people in beach volleyball – Hughes and USC coach Anna Collier – knew it.

"Have you ever visited USC?" Hughes asked. "Have you ever given beach volleyball a thought?"

She was now. And when she returned from Portugal, Collier wasted no time.

"You want to play for USC?" she asked.

Claes certainly did. So bad, in fact, that in practically one sentence, she dropped her commitment to Long Beach, pledged her commitment to USC, and graduated a semester early from El Dorado to enroll as a Trojan in what should have been her second semester of her senior year at El Dorado.

But because Hughes had practiced all fall with Burnham, Claes picked up Alexa Strange, a 6-foot transfer from Nebraska. While Hughes and Burnham dominated the top court – in NCAA sand volleyball, five teams start, ranked one through five, so that the top teams from each school play each other, the No. 2 teams from each school play each other, and so on and so forth – Claes and Strange ran the second. The two teams combined for a 77-11 record that year, but it was just the prelude. With Burnham set for graduation, it was common sense for Collier to pair Hughes with Claes. It was the smartest and easiest coaching move she'd ever have to make.

But they still had the rest of that summer of 2014, when they played in their first Manhattan Beach Open. You could be forgiven if you're surprised by what happened next.

They lost.

Florida State's Jace Pardon had teamed up with Pepperdine's Lara Dykstra – who had qualified for the Manhattan Beach Open a year before with Strange – and smashed Claes and Hughes in straight sets in the second round of the qualifier, 21-12, 21-14. It was humbling and awful and everything Claes and Hughes needed.

"We were nervous," Claes said. "Domestically, it's our biggest tournament. You learn when you win, but you learn so much more when you lose. We really saw what that next level was."

The next level was fast and aggressive and physical. Where college girls are all ball control and crafty shots and grace and fluidity, the professionals were strong and powerful, blasting balls and serving tough, seeming without care if they missed a few. So when they returned to USC for their sophomore year, physically, they were practicing against their teammates, but mentally, they were practicing against imaginary Misty Mays and Kerri Walshes. When they swung, they asked each other if that swing would get past May. If they hit a shot, would it be high enough to stay out of reach of the 6-foot-3 Walsh? If their answer was no to either, they'd grit their teeth and hit the next swing a little harder, the next shot a little crisper.

"We were just trying to set our standards higher than anyone else," Claes said. "That's the big piece that we've been doing. I would also say that playing on the professional tour, you really see the difference between a girl and a woman. They're strong, they're fast, they're aggressive, they're a lot more physical, especially from the college girls. That's a cool thing that we got to see. That first tournament, it was an eye opener."

The mental tricks worked. As sophomores, there was not a single tournament or achievement that Claes and Hughes didn't claim. They won a home tournament. They won the Queen of the Beach. They won the USAV Beach Collegiate Challenge. They won the Pac-12

Invitational. They won 25 straight matches to end the season, the final of which came against Loyola Marymount's Betsi Metter and Sarah Sponcil – who were responsible for two of the duo's three losses on the year – to seal up the team title for USC and the pairs title for Claes and Hughes.

It was everything. It was nothing.

Sara Hughes didn't sit on the wall in Huntington Beach and watch Misty May and dream of success in college. Kelly Claes didn't give up basketball and softball to win a couple tournaments as an amateur. They wanted to be Olympians. First, they needed to be professionals.

The final tournament of the USC season was held on May 3, when they swept Metter and Sponcil for a national title. The next stop on the 2015 AVP Tour was in New York City, on June 16. It was a convenient location for the two. Lauren Hughes, after graduating from Fairfield, took a job in the Big Apple. Sara and Kelly could stay there for free, and they'd take them out to dinner and show them around the most vibrant city in the world.

"So nerve wracking," Claes said of the qualifier. They had only lost three matches since Pardon and Dykstra smoked them in Manhattan a year before. For how much success they had at USC that year, this was the AVP, a different level, and Claes and Hughes had yet to prove they belonged.

Which is exactly what they did.

Neither team in the qualifier scored more than 15 points on USC's precocious stars. They were in the main draw. They were officially on the AVP Tour.

"Beyond stoked," Claes said.

And then, because they were the lowest seed in the main draw, they matched up with the top-seeded team in the whole tournament: April Ross and Jen Fopma. Neither game was close, a 21-15, 21-13 smacking.

Welcome to the AVP Tour, ladies.

"We were living on a high after the qualifier, and we see we get placed against the top seed, and we were like 'Let's go out, let's play hard, let's have fun, we have nothing to lose,'" Claes said. "So we go out there, get our butts handed to us, I just remember them being so physical and us just being like 'Wow, the speed of this game!' We thought we were going fast, and we were not."

"We were just like 'Alright we're going to keep getting after it,'" Hughes said, and it was really quite unbelievable that they did. They took down the ninth-seeded Tealle Hunkus and Sheila Shaw in straight sets and survived a three-setter against No. 6 Ali McColloch and Emily Stockman. Another upset over No. 12 Kerri Schuh and Jessica Stubinski and – holy cow! – they were in the quarterfinals, in a rematch with Ross, a silver medalist in the 2012 Olympic Games, and Fopma.

"Oh my gosh, that was amazing, going back out there, losing to them and then getting a chance to redeem ourselves," Claes said.

Redeeming themselves would have been keeping it close. Redeeming themselves would have been forcing a third set. Redeeming themselves would have been anything but another 21-15, 21-13 blowout. What Hughes and Claes did was shock the No. 1 team in the country. In a match that took just 38 minutes, Hughes and Claes flipped the script on Ross and Fopma, thumping them 21-19, 21-15 to earn a spot in their first AVP semifinal.

"On the last point, I put it down and I look at Kelly and jump in the air like 'What in the world just happened?'" Hughes said. "It was a great feeling. April is a complete stud and an amazing player. We just tried to take it all in."

And then they nearly did it again. Emily Day and Jen Kessy, the second seed, survived a 30-28 marathon of a first game and then dropped the second, 18-21. Fifteen points and Hughes and Claes would be competing in an AVP final, and probably be favored.

It wasn't to be. The veterans won the third, 15-10, and went on to beat Nicole Branagh and Jenny Kropp in the finals. Claes couldn't help but wonder what could have been.

"We were so close!" she said. "That still kills me!"

America loves underdog stories. Claes and Hughes had grabbed the heart of volleyball nation. And while they were disappointed they couldn't sneak away with the third set against Day and Kessy, they knew there was nothing but positives to take away from the trip.

"We went out, and when we talked to each other, we continued to tell each other 'We are at that level.' And in the back of your mind you're always a little nervous playing Olympians. I mean, they're freaking Olympians! Kerri [Walsh] is a three-time gold medalist, it's amazing," Claes said. "To be on the court with them and compete with them, and to be right there was a really eye-opening moment for us."

There was, of course, a contingent of players who considered the tournament a fluke. Anybody can get hot for a couple matches. Let's see if the young'uns can do it again.

"Yea," Hughes said. "Some people thought it was just a phase."

A month later, Hughes and Claes registered for the Manhattan Beach Open, only this time, with a third-place finish in New York to their names, they had enough points to bypass the qualifier as the 14 seed in the 32-team main draw. They did not muster the same magic they had in New York, but they still won three main draw matches, including a 21-11, 21-10 beating over six seed Amanda Dowdy and Heather McGuire, to claim ninth.

A phase?

It was just the beginning.

Amy Grabiec didn't even know Claes and Hughes were signed up for the 2016 AVP New York Open when she agreed to partner up with Lauren Sieckmann. She figured the USC pair would be tired from a jam-packed junior season in Southern California. Surely they wouldn't travel across the country to play in an AVP qualifier.

Wrong.

"All of the qualifier teams were just mad we were there," Claes said. "They were like 'Why are you guys here?' And we just said 'Sorry, we don't have points. We have to pay our dues.'"

"We didn't even know they were playing until we saw the brackets," Grabiec said. "We knew that we wouldn't play them until the second round so we were like 'Well, let's just get through the first one and try our best.'"

Their first one, against Jennifer Dalhausser – wife of gold medalist Phil Dalhausser – and Camie Manwill wound up being a forfeit.

"We didn't even get to warm up," Grabiec griped.

So Grabiec and Sieckmann, who had never played a single set together, went into a match against the best collegiate team in the country, cold and nervous and entirely overwhelmed. It showed.

"Have you ever played a game, and all of a sudden, it's over, and you're like 'What just happened?'" Grabiec asked. "That's what it was like. We had a game plan and we pretty much stuck to it, but they just didn't make a mistake. They would get a point maybe with an ace here, then the next point Kelly would bring it down the middle and score, and then Sara would hit a cut shot. It was always something different. We were constantly trying to process and analyze and change our game but they were doing the exact same thing and they were just way above us.

"Lauren hit this amazing cut shot, like on the one-foot line, and here comes Sara and scoops it up, and we were like 'How the heck did she get that?' She plays defense so well. Like it was an angle block, she was defending the line, and she still picked up a cut shot."

Hughes and Claes smoked Grabiec and Sieckmann 21-11, 21-12, and won their next match, 21-15, 21-16. They were back on the AVP Tour, only unlike their last trip to New York, this main draw was expected. The qualifier, which had once been a cluster of nerves and jitters, was merely an inconvenient formality. Their goals had shifted. They didn't want to simply qualify for the main draw. They wanted to go deep in the main draw.

"We were a little pissed off we were in the qualifier but it was the same mentality: Go out there and kick some butt," Claes said. "We felt like we proved ourselves the last time, so if we play our game, we'll do well."

They did, winning three of their next four matches to make another semifinal, another Sunday on the AVP Tour.

Remember that picture, taken in 1963, of a teenage Bill Clinton meeting JFK, the future meeting the soon-to-be past? The pre-match coin toss of the semifinals in New York of 2016 had a similar vibe.

Standing there was Kerri Walsh, 6-foot-3 inches of sunshine, the G.O.A.T. And there was Sara Hughes, smiling "like a dork" because how else are you supposed to look when you become peers with your idol, when you stand across the net from a three-time gold medalist, the same woman you once shagged balls for as a giggling 8-year-old? And when she was that giggling 8-year-old, all Hughes wanted to do was become Kerri Walsh. As a 21-year-old prodigy, all she wanted to do was step on the same court as her. And in the semifinals in New York City, there she was, flipping a coin against Walsh, hitting shots over and around Walsh, defending hits from from Walsh.

All she wanted to do, in that moment, was dethrone beach volleyball's queen.

"How can we go wrong playing April and Kerri?" Hughes said, and she had a point. Two college girls against perhaps the greatest female athlete of all-time? Who could have expected them to win?

"It was very surreal," Claes said. "We had nothing to lose. We were the underdogs, we were the youngsters. We wanted to prove ourselves. We proved that we could compete with them, but we're obviously not better than them. It was cool to say that we're on a similar level. I would not go as far to say I'm on the same level as them, they've done such amazing things and I'm just starting, but I feel like I can go toe to toe with them."

They did go toe-to-toe, losing just 18-21, 19-21.

Forget the guys' tournament, which was yet another cruise control win for 2008 gold medalist Phil Dalhausser and future Olympian Nick Lucena. In the first set of their semifinal match, against Avery Drost and Billy Kolinske, they led 9-0. Nine-zip? In the semifinals? Sheesh.

So you want to see the future of the sport? Find the blonde and the redhead in the bikinis, not board shorts. Find Betsi Flint, who in Cincinnati in 2015, with Kelley Larsen, became the youngest duo in AVP history to win a tournament. They were a combined 46 years, four months and 27 days. Find Summer Ross – no relation to April – the one who dropped out of Pepperdine, where Larsen ruled, to pursue beach full-time, the one who qualified for her first AVP when she was just 16 years old, who, in 2013 with Emily Day, became the first team in AVP history to make it out of the qualifier to win a title. Find the legions of girls coming out of the college ranks and disrupting the status quo on the pro tours.

That's your future.

"The women's side of the game has eclipsed the men's side of the game," Leonard Armato, the two-time CEO of the AVP Tour, said, "which is really ironic."

Ironic because how many sports can you name, and the immediate image that comes to mind is a female? Golf we think Tiger Woods, not Annika Sorenstam. Basketball? LeBron James or Michael Jordan, not Lisa Leslie. Walsh and May are the exceptions. When the phrase "beach volleyball" is said, it is Walsh and May who immediately come to mind. So it shouldn't be surprising that many point to Hughes and Claes and Summer Ross and Flint and Larsen and the swelling numbers of college women as the ones who will carry the game into its future. Every male player on Tour, after all, once thought the defining characteristic of the sport they grew to love was that it was "a girls sport."

When Hudson Bates, who played on the AVP Tour for eight years, was in eighth grade, his sister dragged him out to a volleyball clinic. He was the only guy there.

Jake Gibb, a three-time Olympian, knew volleyball was huge in Utah when he was growing up, "but for men?" he said. "No. I thought it was a girls sport."

"Still, to this day, all my coworkers give me crap about it, saying 'Oh, you gonna go train with all the girls today?'" said Jon Drake, who made two AVP main draws in 2016.

That's how Mike Brunsting, who would finish the 2016 season second in Rookie of the Year voting, was introduced to the game, too. His older sister, Roxy, was a talented volleyball player at Bonita Vista High School, and when Brunsting enrolled as a freshman, he stood 5-foot-6, thin as a broom handle.

"It's not like I was going to be playing football," he said, and so his father recommended he try out for volleyball.

"I said 'It's a girls sport. I don't really wanna play but I'll do it,'" he recalled. "Still to this day I feel like it's a girls sport."

Many believe that it will remain that way, and by sheer numbers, it's difficult to argue. In the 2014-15 school year, 54,418 boys participated in high school volleyball across 2,287 schools; that same year, 432,176 girls participated in 15,534 schools. It was the No. 2 most popular sport for girls, behind only track and field. It wasn't even in the top 10 for boys, though that makes perfect sense: Only 23 states offer volleyball as a high school sport for boys. All 50, plus Washington, D.C., offer it for girls.

"Honestly, man, it is a girls sport," said Aaron Wexler, a two-time main draw player who founded his own beach club, West Coast Volleyball. "If you look at the numbers, that's what it is, and that's totally cool. So, accurate? Yes. Fair? No."

College is another chapter of the same story: 1,064 NCAA member schools currently sponsor a women's volleyball program, 329 being at the Division I level; only 109 schools did so for the men, and just 23 were Division I. When sand volleyball was introduced as a collegiate sport, 72 schools adopted programs within three years, with another 28 projected to do so by 2020. There are no men's sand programs.

"The girls, that's easy, the stability for growing the game is there," Bates said. "For guys, it's always going to be a back-burner sport, which kind of lends itself to that unique culture, because you have to be really passionate to make it work. There are some kids out there that are literally just – they're going to school at [San Diego State University] just to be able to play beach on the weekends because they love it that much. I think that's kinda what makes it unique and makes it awesome because the guys who need to work to make it to the top. Those guys don't get there by accident. Those guys have been through the shit of it."

The females may have the grassroots, the club teams and the high school programs, the coaching and development through childhood. They may have ten times the amount of college opportunities. But the males have the grind, the rebel culture. They're the ones who just wouldn't conform, wouldn't bow to society's demands that they play football and basketball, that they just put on a suit and tie and get to the office.

They live on passion and, oftentimes, passion alone.

And sometimes, that's just as good.

AVP SAN FRANCISCO

"You're looking at the future of the AVP!"

I t's a shame that the crowd on the morning of June 24, 2016 was sparse, the seats, for the most part, empty. The stadium court in San Francisco, the AVP's fifth event of the year, was, at best, half full and, at best, half enthused.

"Do we have any Brunsting-Frishman fans out there?" AVP emcee March Schuermann called, in reference to the fifteenth-seeded Mike Brunsting and Chase Frishman, who had made it out of the previous day's qualifier. There were a few half-hearted whistles, polite claps.

"And how about the Crabb brothers? Any crabcake fans?"

More polite applause.

Whether they knew it or not – and they certainly did not appear to know it at the moment – the crowd in San Francisco was getting a glimpse into the next generation of male beach volleyball players, the ones tasked with filling the shoes of legends such as Todd Rogers, Phil Dalhausser, John Hyden, Jake Gibb. Here was the 25-year-old Frishman and his 24-year-old blocker, Brunsting. On the other side of the net were 25-year-old Taylor Crabb and his 27-year-old brother, Trevor. The former team was making their ascent up the AVP Tour hierarchy in their rookie seasons; the latter was en route to making their fifth consecutive AVP semifinal. By the end of the season, Frishman would be named Rookie of the Year, an honor that belonged to Taylor Crabb the year before and Trevor Crabb the year before that. The only reason

Brunsting didn't claim the award was because his partner finished one spot ahead of him in the voting at the end of the year.

So if the fans wanted to see who they might be watching on their television sets in the years to come, stadium court on the morning of June 24, 2016 was the place to do it.

"Ladies and gentlemen, you're looking at Tokyo 2020!" Schuermann announced, referring to the 2020 Olympic Games, set to be held in Tokyo, Japan. "You're looking at the future of the AVP!"

But before we look at the future for the men, let's go back.

We're going to a birthday party.

It's either 1999 or 2000. Taylor Crabb can't remember exactly. His local beach in Honolulu, Hawaii, Outrigger Canoe Club, had three beach volleyball courts, though today, the two courts reserved for the adults are not where the action is. Just to the side you'll find what has become affectionately known as the "baby court," which is, as always, teeming with youngsters.

"When you're nine, ten, eleven, all the way to fifteen, that's the court you want to play on," said Riley McKibbin, a Honolulu native, "because you can hit the ball over the net and you don't even have to run down a high line shot because it's like three steps away."

On this occasion, the baby court is packed for Reese Haines's birthday, for which his father has arranged a 2-on-2 tournament. Look there, it's McKibbin and Tri Bourne. They're the geezers of the group – almost teenagers! It explains why they're playing together. And there's Trevor Crabb and Brad Lawson, too. As for the youngsters? That's Taylor Crabb and Riley's kid brother, Maddison. Another set of brothers, Erik and Kawika Shoji have scored invites as well.

Take a snapshot of this precocious crew. You may never see another one like it.

Fast forward now, all the way to 2016. That little birthday crew? They have blossomed into the most formidable group of volleyball players in the world. All in all, in 2016 alone, the nine kids in attendance at that party would go on to combine for eight AVP finals, eight AVP semifinals, four NORCECA (a continental tour featuring teams from north and central America as well as the Caribbean) wins, eight top-five finishes on the FIVB Tour, one beach Olympic qualification, 10 additional AVP main draws, and two indoor Olympic bronze medals.

And that doesn't even include Micah Christensen, another Honolulu boy and one of Taylor Crabb's best friends growing up. Christensen picked up volleyball when he was 14, about five years after Haines's birthday party. By 2016 he had become arguably the best setter in the world, leading the United States indoor team to a bronze medal at the Rio Olympic Games, along with the Shoji brothers.

"It's something people take pride in," said Bourne, a Honolulu native who in 2015 won AVP Team of the Year with Hyden. "In general, you play volleyball in Hawaii and I totally get how it's a girls sport everywhere else, but in Hawaii it's what you do. It's a bigger sport out here. Football is big and volleyball is right behind it. The thing is, no one has ever come out of Hawaii to ever play basketball, but we have had some of the best volleyball players in the world come out of the Outrigger."

Indeed. It would be wrong to say that a single one of them took what could be labeled a traditional path to the AVP Tour, though that might incorrectly suggest that there is such a thing as a "traditional path" in beach volleyball.

Taylor Crabb's route to the AVP is likely the most straightforward of the bunch. A cousin to two-time silver medalist Lindsey Berg (2008, 2012), nephew to 1984 Olympic indoor coach Tony Crabb, and son to a Division I gymnast, Taylor was all but bred to be an athlete. After school, if Taylor wasn't at Outrigger or practice, his father would flip a futon on its side and the Crabbs would play volleyball in the living room. And if it wasn't volleyball it was basketball, or some version of it, anyway.

Taylor was known for, among many things, leading a group of kids to the local elementary school, where the basketball hoops were 8 feet high, and host dunk contests. He wasn't yet a teenager.

"I honestly think that's where he got his athletic coordination," Maddison McKibbin said. "He's always been a very coordinated athlete."

Crabb played basketball and volleyball at Punahou High School, and if that name sounds familiar it should: It is the alma mater of former President Barack Obama. Crabb would graduate a two-time volleyball state champion, landing an offer to play indoor at Long Beach State, where he became a two-time All-American and the 2013 National Player of the Year – all the while being an outside hitter standing not a hair over 6-feet tall.

"What Taylor has done is fucking incredible," Maddison McKibbin said. "But, at the same time, if you look at Taylor as a player, Taylor is one of the most technically sound players on the Tour. If you look at arm swing, ball control, even IQ. Knowing Taylor, it's no surprise. If you saw him play indoor, he's a phenomenal indoor player. Even though some people wrote him off as being too small, he's just a smooth, coordinated volleyball player."

But beach was never really a consideration for Taylor. He liked it, sure, but indoor was his game, his calling. He planned to do it until he was 30 or so and then, when his knees began to ache and his body could no longer absorb the constant beating of a hard surface, he'd transition to beach. It took exactly one year, on an overseas contract in France, for that number to plummet to 23.

"There was something about living nine months in another country by yourself that wasn't really for me, I guess," he said.

He had a decision to make. An indoor team in Puerto Rico had offered him a contract. His brother, Trevor, who had already begun playing on the AVP Tour, offered him an unofficial one: Accrue enough points to be in the main draw and I'll pick you up. But there was no way in hell Trevor was going to fall back into the qualifier to play with little brother.

"It was either sign [the contract in Puerto Rico] or play with my brother on the beach," Taylor recalled. "I said 'Why not? Let's just go for the beach.'"

There was, however, one problem: Taylor still had to qualify. He had done it before, with Trevor in the 2013 Manhattan Beach Open, and the two had even taken a set off of Olympians Phil Dalhausser and Sean Rosenthal in the main draw. But that was two years ago, and Taylor now had zero AVP points to his name. Regardless, he had chosen the beach, and in May of 2015, he made his full-time beach debut, in New Orleans with childhood friend Spencer McLaughlin. They lost in the first round of the qualifier to Kevin Lynch and Connor Hastings. Lynch has never qualified for the AVP Tour, and the last time Hastings did so was in 2009.

"That," recalled Lynch a year later, "is a resume win for me."

"The qualifier is pretty brutal, and we lost like 15-13 in the third, so it came down to a couple points," Taylor said. "And yea, it was the first round, but it doesn't really matter if it's the first or the last round; if you don't qualify, you don't qualify. My mindset didn't really move because of that loss. I knew that the qualifier is brutal. Lots of people don't qualify all the time. Some people, they try to qualify their whole lives, and sometimes they don't. So, I didn't really take it personally. I just tried to improve and learn and make sure I was ready, and we did."

What he did next is wholly unprecedented. Two months later, he took down an AVP champion in Ty Loomis and another main draw regular, Kevin McColloch, to qualify in New York and gave second-seeded John Mayer and Ryan Doherty a mighty scare in the first round of the main draw, ultimately losing 24-22 in the third set. Then came Seattle, in which both of his qualifying wins came in three sets, and that was it. That was all he needed to partner up with Trevor in their first automatic main draw together, in Manhattan Beach.

Enter the Sand Crabbs, the American fan-favorite team of 2015 and 2016.

A loss to their longtime childhood friend, Bourne, in the second round banished them to the long, brutal road of the contender's bracket – "Trevor is still growing a toenail back because the sand was so hot," Taylor said. No problem. Down went Jeremy Casebeer and Derek Olson. Hudson Bates and Dave McKienzie wouldn't score more than 17. They survived a marathon of a match against No. 7 Billy Allen and Brad Keenan (23-25, 21-13, 15-12) and then quickly dismissed sixth-seeded Todd Rogers and Stafford Slick in two. Then came what is likely the best match of the entire 2015 season: A 29-31, 21-17, 16-14 win over the No. 1 seed, Casey Patterson and Jake Gibb.

"Easily the most memorable match I've ever played in," Trevor Crabb said.

Just like that, in their first AVP tournament together as professionals, after seven matches and 17 sets in two days, the Crabbs made their first semifinal appearance. Dalhausser and Nick Lucena smoked the brothers in the semis, 21-14, 21-14, but the message was crystalline: The Sand Crabbs were a bona fide AVP contender.

In less than three months, Taylor made the transition from first-round qualifying knockout to AVP semifinalist.

"It's crazy," Patterson said. "He was such a good player in indoor. It was no surprise he's so good, growing up Hawaii. Everyone had a thought he would be that great but I think he really stepped up and improved. The kid can play at the highest level; it's fun to watch."

In 2016, there was not a single AVP tournament that did not feature the Crabbs in the semifinals or finals, and they finished the year as the top-ranked team on Tour, higher, even, than Olympians Gibb and Patterson and Dalhausser and Lucena.

"It did surprise me," Taylor said of his blink-and-you-missed-it transition from qualifier to No. 1 team on Tour. "I didn't think I'd be in the finals and semifinals in my second year, every tournament."

More surprising than that? That Trevor is playing volleyball at all.

Of all the Punahou kids and Outrigger rugrats, Trevor is the only one who didn't play high school volleyball after his freshman year.

"Trevor didn't really like volleyball," Taylor said. "But he was good at it. I think people were just pressuring him too much to play it, and he has that mindset where people were telling him to do something, so he's going to do something else. So he played basketball."

To his credit, Trevor was good at basketball, though how good depends on whom you ask. Ask Trevor, and he was bound for the NBA, and he even put a hundred bucks on it that he would make the League, something that Riley McKibbin has not – and likely will not – ever let him forget.

"Literally every time we see [Trevor], Riley reminds him about that bet," Maddison McKibbin said.

"Trevor thought he was good but he wasn't, which is basically Trevor in a nutshell," Riley McKibbin said, laughing. "He refused to play high school volleyball because he hated volleyball. We were all just like 'Come on out!' And he said 'Nah, bro, I'm going to the NBA.' So I bet him a hundred bucks he wouldn't go to the NBA and we shook on it."

NBA-caliber? Perhaps not, but he was good enough to lead Punahou's basketball team to a state championship in 2008, which led to an offer from the University of Puget Sound, a small, Division III private school in Tacoma, Washington. He took it, and during his freshman season he helped the Loggers reach the Sweet 16. But just as nine months in France pulled Taylor back to America, a year in Washington was enough to haul Trevor back to be closer with his Hawaiian crew.

"That had an effect on me," he said of the sudden distance between him and his friends and family. "I couldn't really handle that environment in the northwest, just the weather and the atmosphere. It was just tough on me. It was tough going up there, especially your first year out of high school from home. If it had been later on it might not have been that bad, but going to a place totally polar opposite was just a shock."

He wanted out. And he knew just where to go. Despite Trevor not having played indoor volleyball in high school, he had been such a phenomenal athlete on the beach that he was recruited by UCLA and USC anyway. This was a kid who went toe to toe in an open final against Olympians Stein Metzger and Kevin Wong when he was a teenager during a weekend tournament at Outrigger. So when Puget Sound didn't work out, Trevor called up one of the coaches who had recruited him when he was at Punahou. That coach was now at Long Beach State and, yes, he'd love to have Trevor on his team.

Though the prevailing opinion amongst his friends is that Trevor never liked volleyball, it's an inaccurate assertion. Trevor Crabb loved volleyball. He just didn't like it in a gym.

"I always knew," he said, "that beach was going to be my route."

Ask him about his three years – he red-shirted a year after blowing out his shoulder – at Long Beach and you will receive a decidedly lukewarm answer. It was good, not great. Playing with Taylor was fun. Living in California was better than rainy Washington. It served its purpose, which was to prepare Trevor for the beach. And as soon as he graduated, he hit the AVP Tour full-time, initially partnering with Steve VanderWerp for two tournaments before getting picked up by Billy Allen, with whom he would no longer have to qualify. Since becoming an automatic main draw player, through 2016 Crabb has finished outside of the top-10 just once, with 11 appearances in the finals or semifinals in 19 tournaments.

"I would have never told you that Trevor Crabb was going to be one of the top big men," Gibb, a three-time Olympic blocker, said. "It's awesome. It's awesome to see guys getting it done at that size [6-foot-4]."

Meanwhile, in a kitchen in Italy, while Trevor Crabb was discussing partnership possibilities with Allen, two of his friends from youth, Maddison and Riley McKibbin, were wondering if they were finished playing volleyball once and for all.

It had been eight years since Riley McKibbin played competitively on a beach. He was enjoying a successful indoor career, making decent money and seeing the world. But seeing the world can get tiresome after nearly a decade and he was, well, tired.

"I just thought, 'Ok, it's time to move on,'" Riley recalled. Maddison, too, was ready to put his business degree from USC to use. His experience overseas hadn't quite been the same one that Riley had. After graduating from USC, Maddison signed a contract to play in Greece. Two weeks before he left, he fractured his tibia. But he had signed a contract, and he wanted to play volleyball, so off to Greece he went, with a broken tibia and an unwisely expedited rehabilitation. Predictably, it didn't go well.

"My time in Greece," he said, "was a shit show."

His health was, in reality, the least of his concerns.

"If you lose overseas, and you play for a country that's economically not doing very well, the president just won't pay you," he said. "So getting your money is a tough thing to do, and I was kind of done with indoor."

But Riley had signed with a team in Italy and asked Maddison if he'd like to tag along. Which is how, three months later, they found themselves sitting in their kitchen in Italy, pondering their volleyball futures, neither of them particularly thrilled about the prospect of spending the rest of the year overseas, playing a game they didn't much like anymore.

"I had always had more success on the beach than indoor, so we decided 'Hey, let's go home and take a whack on the beach,'" Maddison said. "We had both played in junior international tournaments and always played beach in the summers. We saw Tri and Trevor having success, and we used to always play with them, so we figured why not?"

It sounds simple enough. It, of course, was not. They weren't entirely sure what the state of their beach skills was, so they bought a handful of Wilson volleyballs – the brand used by the AVP – from Costco and exiled themselves to a court in Venice Beach, several zip codes away from any serious players. And so there it was that you could find two professional volleyball players, practicing in Venice Beach, legitimately mortified that someone might see them dusting off the rust of a game they hadn't played for the better part of a decade.

"We couldn't even hit it over the net," Riley said. "The transition from indoor to the beach is so hard. We're both indoor players, and making that switch is a lot harder than people think."

After a few weeks in Venice, the McKibbins were brave enough to enter an open CBVA tournament in Hermosa Beach. They were knocked out in just three matches.

Regardless of their quick exit, "the next three days, I was bedridden," Riley said. "I swear to God, I couldn't move. I had my girlfriend bring me food. The muscles you use for beach and indoor are completely different. It's not like riding a bike, but it's not like we were learning it for the first time. Setting is a totally different skill. It took me forever to learn how to set on the beach."

But Riley didn't have forever. He had until July 15, 2015, when he and Maddison were set to play in their first AVP event together, in New York City.

The Hawaiian culture is a close-knit one, valuing, above all else, family. If you know a Hawaiian, or have seen any movie featuring Hawaii, you have likely heard the term ohana, which translates roughly to "family" and is ubiquitous in the culture. Which is why the phone call that the brothers received from their aunt on the night of July 14 rendered the typically convivial duo rather solemn, and turned their preparation on the eve of their professional beach volleyball debut into closing down a bar in Brooklyn called Baby's All Right, sipping water and juice, thinking about anything but beach volleyball.

"Nana," their aunt on the other end of the phone, told them, "is dying."

"It was," Riley said, "a really traumatic event for all three of us."

Which made what happened the next day that much sweeter.

"We kind of looked at that qualifier as getting your driver's license, like we're probably going to fail the first time, you know?" Riley said. "Plus, we're in New York, and we're babysitting our little brother, [Jameson], and we actually made him our coach, a fifteen-year-old kid with braces, so we just put no pressure on ourselves. Who cares? Let's just see what we can do. It was almost guaranteed we weren't going to make it."

Only they did make it. They thumped Chris Fleming and Timmy Epps 21-11, 21-13 in the first round, which preceded a matchup with their childhood friend, Brad Lawson, and Adam Roberts in the second. There, the McKibbins delivered what may be considered the upset of the qualifier, winning 15-4 in the third set to move onto the final round, against New York native Mark Burik and his 6-foot-9 partner, Curt Toppel. The McKibbins won in straight sets, 21-19, 21-19, making their first main draw in their first try, in a tournament they in no way expected to contend, less than 24 hours removed from the death of their grandmother.

"It was such a surreal event for us," Riley said. "It was our first tournament, we had somehow beat all these good teams and qualified. After all the indoor, and the good matches I've had, the high school state championships, playing overseas – that win right there was by far my most memorable. That was my greatest accomplishment. Our grandmother had just passed away, which made it huge for us. I don't want to say we won it for her, but there was that factor there. And we also upset a few teams we never thought we'd beat going into it. We just didn't expect to make it that far and all of a sudden, we're in the AVP on our first try. And Jameson, our youngest brother, was there. We made him our coach the rest of the tournament, so it was like a family victory in so many ways. And that kind of catapulted us. It got us hooked."

And by the final tournament of the 2016 season, in Chicago, there was Maddison and Riley McKibbin, taking ninth out of 24 main draw teams, and Trevor and Taylor Crabb placing third alongside Tri Bourne.

Five Hawaiian kids, all younger than 28, raised within walking distance of one another on the courts at the Outrigger Canoe Club, galvanizing a power shift on the AVP Tour.

"We've all come a long way," Riley said, "from the baby court."

Chase Frishman's story does not begin at the Outrigger Canoe Club. He did not grow up playing against Kevin Wong and Stein Metzger, though he did grow up, as he likes to say, "on the sand, pretty much out of the womb." Frishman's father, John, played on the AVP in his younger days, and his mother, Kristi, was a former club skier for UCLA. As soon as their little boy could stand up, he was playing volleyball. But there was also a small problem: Chase was tiny. When he enrolled in Dana Hills High School in Dana Point, California, he was 5-foot-2 and didn't yet tip the scales at 100 pounds.

"All I did," he said, "was work and scrap and play defense."

And the boy could scrap. And holy cow could he play defense. The University of California, San Diego called and asked him if he might want to play libero for the Tritons, and it was an offer that proved fairly prescient. In the three months between his graduation from Dana Hills and his first day of classes at UCSD, Frishman sprouted up to 6-foot-1. It wasn't height necessarily built for an opposite or outside hitter, but it helped Frishman finish his four-year career with 674 career digs, which ranks second all-time at UCSD. A professional team in Tsvjona, Switzerland called shortly after. They needed an outside hitter. Would Chase be up for it? He didn't much have a choice – a childhood friend from Laguna Beach, Tom Ribarich, who was also on the team, had already committed Frishman. He was going to Switzerland.

"I was like 'Are you kidding me, dude? I've never played outside!'" Frishman said. "And then I get there, and I'm the only foreigner, I'm the only guy getting paid. It was kind of an awkward situation. They were like 'Who is this little guy? He's tiny, can't block, he can only rip it off a block.'"

But he could still play some damn good defense, and the coaches offered Frishman a contract to play libero for them the next season. The issue with that offer, however, was that, to hedge against attrition, Frishman was not the only libero they offered. By the time Frishman committed to return to Switzerland for another year, they had already signed another libero.

"I was kind of left with my ass out," he said.

So here was Frishman, a 23-year-old kid from Southern California, armed with a degree in communications he didn't plan to use, cut from a professional team he had never actually expected to play for, direction-less. He did what he had always done: He went to the beach. The timing of it all was impeccable. A teammate from UCSD, Mike Brunsting, was moving from San Diego to Lake Forest. He gave Frishman a call, wondering if he wanted to start training on the sand. At the time, Frishman had been practicing with a former Stanford football and volleyball player named Myles Muagututia, and Brunsting had been playing in AVP qualifiers with Jake Dietrich, a former outside hitter at UC Santa Cruz. On a winter afternoon at Doheny Beach, Frishman and Muagututia, exceptional athletes in their own right, played a few matches against Brunsting and Dietrich, and "it was just a whole new level," Frishman said. "I was like 'What the hell?' They were cutting us up, hammering balls. They had been training and they played AVP the whole year before, so they had seen that competition. It was a reality check."

But Dietrich was moving away from volleyball, settling into a full-time job and preparing to marry his longtime girlfriend, a former Clemson volleyball player named Lisa Jedicka. Brunsting needed a partner, and he didn't particularly want to play defense, either. He and Frishman had been teammates for three years at UCSD, so it made perfect sense to ask his old libero to play defense behind his block.

It was the decision that kept his volleyball career alive.

Just three years before, Brunsting was prepared to remove himself from the game. His great grandfather had once been the head of dermatology at a hospital, uncle a doctor in an emergency room, aunt a general surgeon.

"I thought that [the medical field] was my path," he said. In 2014, as a senior at UCSD, when he would be named the team's MVP, he began applying to medical schools, sending applications to essentially all the UC schools and the Oregon Health and Sciences University, among "about five-hundred million" others. But the application process is not a swift one, and while Brunsting was waiting to hear back, he figured he may as well train on the beach.

"I wanted that experience," he said, "And if I could feel myself plateauing, then that's when I feel like I would need to call it quits."

The plateau wouldn't happen. In 2014, playing in just his second qualifier, this one in Huntington Beach with Paul Araiza, a veteran player and San Diego native, as the 15-seed, Brunsting qualified, beating Adam Cabbage and Jake Rosener in the final round, 21-15, 23-21 to make main draw.

"I was 100 percent surprised," Brunsting said. "We were playing Adam Cabbage and Jake Rosener, who I know now, and I think it's funny looking back being so naïve, but I truly was. Everybody was serving me every ball. It was funny, man. I didn't really expect it. We got a great draw in the second round, so that was convenient. And in the third round, Paul was playing lights out, and I was just doing what I could. It was very real in the moment, and I guess I was just surprised that we won. I think I didn't have a good idea of what it was that I got into.

"I was in volleyball for eight years and the AVP is just, you know, it's not that big, even for volleyball players. I didn't know I was gonna make over a thousand dollars, I didn't know how hard people work to get to that point a lot of the time. I didn't really know. I remember Russ Marchewka coming up to me and shaking my hand and saying

'Welcome to the AVP' and I'm just thinking 'Wow, this is crazy!' It was super exciting and I had confidence in my volleyball abilities. It's not like I didn't have a volleyball pedigree and I just picked up the sport. I had been playing for a while at a pretty high level and I when I got into Huntington I was like 'Wow, that's great.' It's still cool to finish that high, thirteenth in the nation. I was super motivated coming out of that tournament, and it was an easy decision to make to try and play pro instead of grind it out in medical school."

But during the 2015 season, Brunsting struck out. In the season-opening event in New Orleans, partnered with Dietrich, he lost to Tim and Brian Bomgren in the second round of the qualifier. At the next stop in Seattle, the two were knocked out in the first qualifying round by the McKibbins. Partnered with Spencer McLaughlin in Manhattan, it was a second-round qualifier exit and two weeks later, in Chicago with Miles Evans, he was bounced by Kevin McColloch and Matt Motter in the third round of the qualifier. Despite training full-time and putting a promising medical career on hold, Brunsting didn't qualify for a single tournament all season.

"It was freakin' rough, man," Brunsting said. "I was told that it was a very real possibility that I don't qualify, that a lot of guys don't. And I was like 'Ok, that's a possibility, my goal is to qualify for half of them.' I thought that was realistic. I played with a couple different guys and I just felt like I never got anything going. It was frustrating because I didn't know how to get better, I didn't know what to get better at. I knew what my goals were, and it was very difficult to not have, like in college or ever before, a coach telling you this is what you need to do, this is how it's done, so that was really hard. So I felt kind of helpless in my improvement so I just had to think about it. I knew I wanted to try again because I was so close. It's not like I was getting smashed in these games. I was close, so I knew it was a possibility I could do well, but it was hard. It was just kind of a grind and I was banging my head against the wall and I couldn't really break through."

Skill-wise, Brunsting may not have known what he needed to improve upon, but he did know one aspect of his life he had to change if he were to take this seriously: He needed to move. For years, he had trained with the same group – Araiza, Derek Olson, Alejandro Parra, occasionally Matt Olson and McColloch. Something had to change. So in 2016 he moved to Lake Forest and dialed up Frishman, and the two, after a few practices, decided to play an AVP Next – a developmental series of tournaments for up and coming players – that February.

They didn't lose a single set.

"That's when I knew that there was so much stuff Chase and I could do to get better from a team dynamic," Brunsting said. "It felt like a new direction and I was much, much more motivated. That was super exciting and kind of got the engines going again."

By the fifth tournament of the year, in San Francisco, Frishman and Brunsting made four main draws. They upset longtime main draw teams like Hudson Bates and Mark Burik, Marty Lorenz and Adam Roberts, Araiza and Parra. In New York, no team scored more points on Phil Dalhausser and Nick Lucena than Brunsting and Frishman. In San Francisco, they stood toe to toe with the Crabbs, losing 18-21, 18-21. But beyond the wins and the prize money, it was the difference in mindset that proved most monumental: Brunsting expected to win.

"It's hard," he said. "The season goes from May all the way to September, so our expectations change. They go up then they go down, they go left then they go right just because of how you did the day before. Maybe you hit 50 balls out and you're like 'I can't play volleyball anymore.' It's a roller coaster of emotions but I'm super happy with how we did. I think Mike in January would not have expected this at all, especially with Chase, who I'd never played with before. You don't just walk into your first year on the AVP and qualify five out of seven times. I don't think I would have foreseen that type of success."

The success they achieved is the envy of every qualifying team, for after San Francisco, Brunsting and Frishman had alas eclipsed the golden threshold: They worked their way up the ladder, earning enough points that they were out of the qualifier and straight into main draw for the final two events of the season, in Manhattan Beach and Chicago.

"Man, I can't tell you how nice it is to just rest your legs on a Thursday," Brunsting said. "It was just exciting and Manhattan is a big tournament for everybody and we were just excited to have that extra edge on everybody. It was huge. I didn't care that I was in the sun all day. I got to rest my legs and hang out with the people I love and rub it in everyone's face that I didn't have to qualify."

Their success was noted by their main draw peers. Guys like Bourne admitted that he "was very impressed with Chase." Casey Patterson, who was the first big time player to welcome Frishman and Brunsting into his training group, called the two "ballers."

"It reminds me of when I was back in the qualifier and everyone was playing because there was an actual future in volleyball," Patterson said. "That's all this is. It's the next wave of guys who have seen that it's possible and they're doing it. These guys, four years ago, would have played [indoors] overseas for a little then got a job and quit. But now these guys can actually do it. Especially Chase, that guy is out there every day. I was like the Chase when I was younger, 'I'm gonna be at the beach all day long, work my way up the ladder.' It's good to see, it's like 'Dude, that was me!'"

But they are not Casey Patterson. Not yet, though truth be told, Jake Gibb has been waiting for this moment. He sees the Crabbs and the McKibbins, Tri Bourne and Chase Frishman and Mike Brunsting. The new generation is on its way in. His, the one that earned an Olympic gold medal in 2000 and another in 2008, is on its way out. And he's ok with that.

"I've been waiting for this for a long time," he said. "Throughout my career, I'm always watching, thinking 'What big guys are coming to end my job?'"

He has seen plenty who have had the potential, guys like Robbie

Page, a 7-foot blocker in his early 20s, and "they're out there, just crushing balls, and I'm thinking 'Man, I'm just trying to hold onto my spot. For whatever reason, guys just fall off. Some guys just fall off."

Page already has. It is nothing short of remarkable that Gibb never did.

Gibb's path to volleyball is a decidedly unique one. Raised in Bountiful, Utah, the youngest of 11 children, Jake was tall and athletic, a perfect fit for the basketball court. He wouldn't pick up a volleyball until he was a senior at Bountiful High School, and even then, it wasn't anything serious. He'd mess around in his backyard with his family – the Gibbs could have 6-on-6 games in the backyard if they so chose – until the grass was worn into a crunchy brown, but it was far from the teachings that his current peers were receiving in California. Volleyball was a fun little side sport to play with the family, and it remained that way for the next year, when he took a Mormon mission trip and didn't see a volleyball for a year.

When he returned, however, he wanted to see if he could put his athleticism to use – on a volleyball court, not a basketball court. In his first year, he ascended from the novice tournaments to open, the highest level, "just figuring it out," he said. And he certainly would figure it out, and fast. Gibb would go on to finish the next three seasons as the top-ranked player in the state of Utah, losing only one match in his final two years.

In 2000, a man named Mike Daniel took notice of the kid and asked if Gibb might want to play AVP tournaments with him. Daniel was a solid player himself, a former outside hitter at BYU and Colorado State who was the No. 1 ranked player in Utah from 1994-96. He would foot the travel bill and entry. All Gibb had to do was show up. So off they went, flying to Chicago and Santa Barbara, Muskegon and Belmar, finishing the season in Manhattan Beach, a tournament that Gibb would eventually win, as of this writing, three times with three different partners. They qualified twice, in Muskegon and Belmar, and that, as Gibb says, "was the start of it." He had his taste. He wanted to pursue this still-foreign sport, and during the tournament in Belmar, in which Gibb and Daniel would qualify and finish 25th, he learned how.

Daniel and Gibb were in the players' tent when they ran into Mike Whitmarsh, a silver medalist in the 1996 Atlanta Olympic Games with Mike Dodd. Daniel asked Whitmarsh for any tips or advice on how to progress in his career. Whitmarsh asked them where they were from, and when Daniel replied "Utah," Whitmarsh laughed and replied, "Well, that's your problem."

That was Gibb's solution. He was moving to California. And in 2002, he did, with a set of conditions. Gibb was a newlywed, having married his high school sweetheart, Jane, in 2000. They were young and ambitious and riding the highs of a young relationship. Jane agreed on a two-year window: If her husband could make a living playing beach volleyball within two years, he could stick with it; if not, Gibb says, "I'd get into business and be a normal career man."

In truth, that is exactly what both Gibbs expected to happen. But as it can sometimes go in life, "it was just one thing after another," he said. A win in Austin in 2004 led to a partnership with Stein Metzger, an Olympian in the Athens Games, in 2005. In their first year as partners, they won four AVPs, finished second in three others and made the semifinals in another five. In just their first year as partners, they finished as the No. 1 team on Tour.

Gibb had all but trashed his initial goals, the ones where his only requirement was to simply make enough money to avoid getting a real job. New ones inevitably began to form. His first year with Metzger changed his thinking. With the success the two were having on the American tour, Gibb wondered what they might be capable of on the international scene. And Metzger, having already been an Olympian, had the points to pull them into FIVB main draws. So off they went, to Germany and Portugal, France and Austria, Brazil and Mexico and

South Africa, making three podiums, finishing the international season as the No. 4 seed in their final international tournament.

"That," Gibb says, "is when I began to realize that Olympics were a legitimate possibility."

In July of 2008, Gibb was sitting in a plane in Moscow, Russia. The plane rumbled as it taxied around the jetway. Phones were supposed to be off but Gibb couldn't help but leave it on for just...one...more... second. There was too much at stake. As the plane picked up speed, preparing for takeoff, his Blackberry lit up with a message.

"Congratulations, Olympian," it read.

The plane erupted. Jane, his wife, began crying. The Olympics were no longer just a legitimate possibility. They were a reality.

"It was really emotional," Gibb said.

And it would unintentionally remain that way. Gibb didn't have enough service to reply or confirm what he had just read. He couldn't be 100 percent sure that he and his partner for the previous two seasons, Sean Rosenthal – Metzger had dropped Gibb for Mike Lambert at the end of the 2005 season – were indeed Olympians. So over the next 12 hours on the flight from Russia to the U.S., Gibb would stare at his Blackberry, waiting for the occasional bar of service and attempt a swift reply, which, of course, would be denied. He'd have to wait. But when he landed, he was able to validate that initial message: Jake Gibb was officially an Olympian, set to compete alongside Rosenthal in the 2008 Beijing Games.

"It was a surreal moment," he said. "We couldn't believe it was real."

But it was. Phil Dalhausser and Todd Rogers had long since locked up the spot as the No. 1 American team, leaving the second – in the Olympics, there is a limit to two teams per country – open to either Gibb and Rosenthal or Casey Jennings and Matt Fuerbringer. It came down to the final international tournament preceding the Beijing Olympics, in Moscow, which Jennings and Fuerbringer essentially needed to win, or at the very least, make finals. They wouldn't, finishing ninth. Gibb and Rosenthal, just two years into their partnership, were going to the Olympics.

"When Jake and I got together we said we wanted to play on the world tour and AVP. The Olympics were brought up but it wasn't our top goal," Rosenthal said. "But it was definitely brought up then, and after 2006 we knew we could make a good run."

They weren't delusional. They knew Dalhausser and Rogers were all but a lock. Their main competition would be Lambert and Metzger and Fuerbringer and Jennings. At the end of the 2007 season, Gibb and Rosenthal held a slim lead over Lambert and Metzger and a monstrous one over Jennings and Fuerbringer. Between the 2007 and 2008 seasons, Lambert had surgery on a balky knee and, as Rosenthal says, "never recovered," retiring from the international scene. With Metzger and Lambert out, only Jennings and Fuerbringer remained, though the gap between them was so wide that "we knew we had it locked up," Rosenthal said.

The funny part about the Olympics: It is not the best beach volleyball tournament. Not by a long shot. Each country is limited to two teams, meaning that powerhouses Brazil, America, Germany, Russia can only send its two best teams, despite its next two – or three or four – being exponentially better than, say, the top team from Africa. But still: It's the Olympics. Like swimming and track, most of the world view the Olympics as a quadrennial sport, one that pops up on TV for a few weeks every four years, becomes an NBC-ratings booster, and disappears again for another four years. But during those two weeks, the sport commands the attention of the entire world. In 1996, the quarterfinals, semifinals and finals were all sold out. Ditto with Beijing in 2008 and London in 2012. In Rio in 2016, where beach volleyball is as big as the NBA or NFL in America, matches began at 8 a.m. and didn't end until midnight, with spectators filling the stadium throughout.

"It's the biggest tournament for beach volleyball," Dalhausser says. "You go down in history. Everybody will remember who won a gold medal at the Olympics, but nobody will remember who won a gold in Marseille in 2009, you know?"

So even for a guy like Rosenthal, whom Gibb has labeled "the coolest guy on the planet," the magnitude of a player's first Olympics is a moment of rapture.

"Right before our first match," Rosenthal recalls, "I get a call from a friend. He said 'Y'all still playing?' I said 'Yeah, we're still playing. Why?' And he goes 'It's pouring rain!' I looked outside and it was raining the hardest I've ever seen. So that was pretty cool, we just had fun, you know? It's still one of the funnest matches I've ever played."

"Oh my gosh," said Jake's wife, Jane, "that match was unbelievable. So much fun."

It was an auspicious start for the hot young Americans. Gibb and Rosenthal won all three of their pool play matches and then took down Spain's Pablo Herrera and Raul Mesa in the first round of elimination. They would play the winner of the match that followed, between Brazil's Emanuel Rego and Ricardo Santos, then the No. 1 team in the world, and Russia's Dmitri Barsouk and Igor Kolodinsky.

The Russians were good – anyone who makes the Olympics is – but not Brazilian good. For the next hour, Gibb and Rosenthal were massive Russian fans. And it almost worked. Russia had two swings in the second set to win the match. Santos blocked them both. Brazil held on in the third set to win the match, 18-21, 25-23, 15-12.

"And sure enough," Rosenthal says, "they played great ball against us like they always do."

Rego and Santos beat Rosenthal and Gibb in straight sets in the quarterfinals, 21-18, 21-16, leaving Gibb and Rosenthal in fifth. It's not that they were satisfied, but they were both young and brimming with promise, easy to peg as medal favorites in the 2012 London Games.

"We were ready to come back, 2012," Rosenthal said. "But that was a long way away in beach volleyball. It was brought up but not – we wanted to win more tournaments. That was always the number one thing: winning tournaments."

And Rosenthal and Gibb knew how to win tournaments. But no one – no one – knew how to win tournaments like Dalhausser and Rogers.

The Rogers-Dalhausser partnership began, as Gibb's career had, with a little serendipity. In 2005, Dalhausser and Nick Lucena had moved from South Carolina to Santa Barbara, where they jumped in with a training group that included 2004 Olympians Jeff Nygaard and Dax Holdren and Rogers and Sean Scott. Each partnership was wildly successful: Dalhausser and Lucena won in Austin in 2005, marking their first Tour victory; Holdren and Nygaard made the semifinals or finals in seven of the first eight events of the year; and Rogers and Scott closed out the year with three straight tournament wins.

Still: Rogers wanted more.

"The game was getting bigger," he said. "I wanted a bigger blocker."

His first option was Gibb. The two liked each other, and Gibb had already enjoyed tremendous success with Metzger, who had dropped him for Lambert. But they both wanted to play right side, which proved to be a deal breaker, and Gibb wound up picking up Rosenthal instead. Next on the list was Lambert, the 2004 AVP MVP and one half of the AVP Team of the Year alongside Karch Kiraly. Lambert never called him back, presumably because he had already agreed to play with Metzger.

Not knowing where else to go, Rogers turned to the media, specifically Don Patterson, a longtime writer for the Los Angeles Times and editor of DiG Magazine who had written a feature on Dalhausser.

"I was sitting there, singing Phil's praises, and Don said 'Maybe you should pick him up,'" Rogers said. "And I was like 'Man, he's third on my list, but he has that upside. He is a little rawer than Jake Gibb and doesn't have the finishes of Mike Lambert but he's got this upside.'"

That upside was enough to convince Rogers to give Dalhausser a shot. It was not enough, however, for Rogers to ignore Dalhausser's lax attitude.

"I basically said, 'You're lazy, you don't really want to work hard but you have a tremendous amount of talent,'" Rogers recalls. "'If you want to play with me I want to go full bore and I want you to buy in – the weightlifting, the workouts, all the training, three to four times per week, working on things to get better.'"

Dalhausser admits as much. But, lazy or not, two instances in particular swayed Rogers for good. The first came in practice, on a totally meaningless play, though that's also what made it so impactful.

"I hit a ball and Phil was blocking and Nick dug it but he dug it way off the court and Phil ran it down, pulled it back into the court and Nick sent it back in, and we ended up getting the point in practice but it was 'Holy crap!'" Rogers said. "I remember talking to Sean, and Sean was smaller, six-foot-five, and strong and fast, and I told him 'Dude, you're the only guy I've ever seen go run and get that ball. All these other big guys can't do that. That was impressive.' And he said 'Yeah, that was impressive.'"

The next came in June of 2005, at an FIVB Grand Slam event in Berlin. Scott had broken his pinky, and Rogers needed a quick fill-in. Dalhausser obliged, and with just one day of practice as partners, they finished seventh, beating a pair of German teams ranked in the top-10 in the world as well as Americans Dain Blanton and Kevin Wong. It was important for a number of reasons, though one in particular: Rogers and Scott, for all the success they reaped in America, had never medaled on the world stage. With one day of practice, he and Dalhausser nearly pulled it off.

So when Dalhausser returned to California after a brief winter vacation in January of 2006, he did so "with the mindset thinking 'I'm going to do exactly what [Todd is] going to do.' He showed me how to be a professional athlete, I guess. I was one year out from Myrtle where you just partied and played volleyball and that was not Todd's idea of playing beach volleyball."

Prior to his partnership with Rogers, Dalhausser had played in 30 AVP tournaments and won one. Over the next three seasons with Rogers, he would play in 48 and win 29.

"We had this formula and teams just played into this formula," Dalhausser said. "They would serve Todd and I just had to worry about setting him and he just had to worry about siding out. I could focus on bombing serves and blocking balls. I was our point scorer and that was my focus and anytime he would scoop a ball and put it away it was a bonus and every time I went over on two it was to help him out a little which was another little bonus."

"That team," said Matt Olson, who lost to Dalhausser and Rogers in the 2007 Hermosa Beach final, "was ridiculous."

In the lead-up to the Beijing Olympics, the two had won 15 of their past 21 events and had accumulated a record of 94-8, a kind of success matched only by the American women, Misty May-Treanor and Kerri Walsh-Jennings. Not even Gibb and Rosenthal could stop the Thin Beast and The Professor. And then the damndest thing happened: In the first round of pool play in the 2008 Olympics, the unstoppable force came to a crashing halt.

The Olympics come around twice a decade, and they do so with much pomp and circumstance, with celebration and ceremony, unrivaled pressure to go with never-before-felt pride of playing for one's country on the biggest stage in competitive sport. It is more than a competition. It is an experience. It's just that sometimes those experiences don't bode well for the competition.

Like the Opening Ceremony.

Beijing's Opening Ceremony has been labeled, almost unanimously by news outlets, as the best in the history of the Olympic Games. More than 100 heads of state came to see the extravaganza, which featured more than 15,000 performers, lasted more than four hours, and cost more than $100 million. So no, Dalhausser was not going to miss them, even if he had to play the next morning. Rogers participated in the Parade of Nations and then bailed. He and Gibb were in the hotel by 11. Dalhausser stumbled in at 4 in the morning.

They played a few hours later.

So what? All he had to do was bomb serves and set Todd, right? No real reason to have fresh legs. And besides, their first-round match was against Latvia's Martins Plavins and Aleksandrs Samoilovs, the No. 23-seed. The last time Dalhausser and Rogers had played them, in Brazil in 2007, the Americans pasted them 21-8, 21-14. Dalhausser readily admits that he "took them lightly." He also readily admits that the Latvians gave him a bit of a shock when they served him every single ball, something that no team had ever done. It just so happened to be the day after Dalhausser was on his feet until the wee hours of the morning, marveling at the glitz and glamour of the Opening Ceremony.

"It's funny," Dalhausser says. "It's almost like they sensed a weakness."

They did. And it worked, as Latvia shocked the world with a 21-19, 21-18 upset of the Americans.

"It was brutal," Rogers says. "It sucked. No other way to say it. It was a serious bummer. It kind of was because Phil was terrible that game. He was exhausted and you could tell; he couldn't jump, his legs were basically dust."

Yet here is the secret that few realize about that loss: Something greater was at work. Latvia's upset ultimately paved the way to what would become the easiest road to the gold medal match for the Americans. Dalhausser and Rogers pounded Argentina and Switzerland in straight sets in their next two matches, claiming the No. 2 seed out of Pool B. It so happened that in the 2008 Olympics, the No. 2 seed out of Pool B was the perfect spot to be. Had Dalhausser and Rogers won their opening match, as they should have, they would have matched up with Brazilians Fabio and Marcio in the quarterfinals, and then Rego and Santos in the semifinals. Instead, their bracket was marked by a who's who of underdogs. To get to the gold medal match, all they had to do was avoid another seismic upset.

Easy, right?

'Course not.

Because here, in the opening round of bracket play, was Switzerland's Martin Laciga and Jan Schnider, bombing three straight jump serve aces to open up a 6-1 lead in the third set after stealing a 23-21 win in the second.

"I remember looking at Phil, going 'Well, if he keeps serving like that, we're toast,'" Rogers recalled. "He was just playing that well, and you can't move Phil over to the line because this guy could serve whatever spot."

Laciga came back to Earth, popping a passable serve that the Americans sided out. Dalhausser blocked him on the ensuing point. And then Laciga made the mistake that possibly cost the Swiss the match: He called a timeout.

"Freaked out," Dalhausser said. "It was way too early."

Because Dalhausser blocked another. And then another. Suddenly it was 6-5. Suddenly, arguably the best male team the world had ever seen was gathering momentum, and there was nothing the Swiss had left in the tank to stop it.

"After that," Rogers says, "we were all good." And they were, pulling out a 15-13 win, finishing the match on a 14-7 run.

From there, as Dalhausser likes to say, "the stars just aligned." For how else can you explain the Germans stunning top-seeded China in straight sets? And then, one round later, Georgia slipping past the Dutch.

Georgia? In the semifinals of the Olympics?

"Literally the best thing we could have had," Dalhausser said.

By the time Dalhausser and Rogers worked their way to the gold medal match, winning their semifinal 21-11, 21-13, the highest-seeded team they had to play was eighth-seeded Germany in the quarterfinals. Meanwhile, on the other side of the bracket, Fabio and Marcio battled with their fellow Brazilians, stunning Rego and Santos in straight sets in the semifinals.

Another blessing.

"Ricardo and Emanuel – those were the guys we were doing battles with," Dalhausser says. "Fabio and Marcio were kind of limping into the tournament."

So yes, the stars had aligned. The cosmos in perfect rotation. The Earth balancing on its axis just so. A late night at the Opening Ceremony had engendered a serendipitous loss to a team they should have never lost to, which resulted in an easy draw, which begat a Swiss meltdown in the third set, which led to a path paved by a monumental upset in the second round, and another in the third, and another in the fourth. And now, here were Dalhausser and Rogers, playing a struggling Brazilian team that was chronologically the last team to qualify for the Olympics.

And they were getting clobbered.

Dalhausser missed his first serve of the match. The Americans went down 2-1. Not an emergency. And then Fabio blocked Rogers, and Dalhausser set him way off the net on the next. Rogers erred. Then Dalhausser erred. Anther block.

6-1.

6-1? Wasn't this the Brazilian team the Americans wanted?

Years later, Rogers would recall thinking that "we knew we had it won" when they saw Rego and Santos go down. But in that moment, they were only assured a medal, and the color didn't appear to be gold.

Dalhausser shanked a pass. Meanwhile, Fabio, the blocker, was passing and siding out, making it look easy.

9-5.

And then Dalhausser showed the sold-out crowd in Beijing why he was, at the time, considered the best beach volleyball player on the planet. Block. Eighty mile per hour jump serve that produced a dig and a point in transition. Block.

Timeout Brazil.

Another block that landed just an inch wide. No matter. It was 11-10 Brazil, though the Americans, with all that momentum, may as well have been leading 11-0. Rogers, whatever nerves he may have had now gone, sided out perfectly the remainder of the match. Cut shots. Swings. Pounding it off Fabio's block. Back and forth it went.

20-20.

A blink-and-you-missed-it cover off a Fabio block set up Dalhausser for a swing and he buried it. Game point with the Thin Beast at the service line. Fabio slipped a line shot by Dalhausser. Rogers returned the favor.

22-21.

Game point number three.

A shanked pass from Fabio produced a set way off the net, and a swing directly into it. First set, Americans.

But this was the Olympics, and after everything Dalhausser and Rogers had been through to get to this point – losing to Latvia, coming back against the Swiss, coming back against the Brazilians in the first set – there was only one way this match was going to go: Three sets. After Rogers and Dalhausser raced to a 13-10 lead, you could have been forgiven for changing the channel. This one's over. Let's check in at the Water Cube to watch Michael Phelps rake in another gold medal – eight! – and etch another world record. But it wasn't over. Dalhausser and Rogers were the No. 1 team in the world, but they did not possess the uninterrupted dominance of Phelps.

The Brazilians charged back. Ace, ace, dig, transition point. A miraculous swing from Rogers well off the net kept the score tied at 14 apiece, but the momentum had swung heavily in Brazil's favor, where it would stay. A block by Fabio made it 17-15, and another, on Dalhausser, 18-15.

Timeout.

No use.

Brazil would play flawless volleyball to claim the second set, digging balls, blocking balls, abusing Dalhausser's block, watching as Dalhausser buried a jump serve into the net to hand Brazil the second set, 21-17.

To three they went.

But here it is vital to note something that Karch Kiraly, a gold medalist himself in 1996 who was commentating the match, said late in the first set: "The talk on the World Tour, the memo for 2008: serve Fabio. Make him work. He's going to get tired. It's going to affect his blocking."

Kiraly, as always, was prescient. Fabio sprayed a pass to begin the third and then hit the net on a swing well off the net. Dalhausser scooped it easily and pounded it off Fabio's block. Fabio lay in the sand, gasping, heaving, caked in sweat and sand.

"Wear him out," Kiraly urged.

Dalhausser blocked him straight down on the next point. The Americans jumped out to a 3-0 lead. They stayed on Fabio, and soon Marcio began melting down, too, berating his blocker for a set that was too low in transition, which produced a hitting error. And then he was called for double-contact on a set of his own. The wheels were coming off.

Another block from Dalhausser.

The Americans hadn't lost a match that went to three sets since 2006. This was not going to be the first. Another block. Make it another. One more for good measure.

9-1 Americans.

It was over.

"We're seeing the cumulative effect," Kiraly said, "of going play after play after play at Fabio."

Brazil had nothing left in the tank.

At 13-4, the giant Brazilian bombed another one out of bounds. And on the next point, it ended the only way it could have, Dalhausser spreading that pterodactyl wingspan and pressing over the net, left hand smothering Fabio's final swing, batting the ball straight down.

15-4 Americans. Gold medal, Americans.

Delirium. Rogers and Dalhausser collapsed into one another and crashed onto the sand. Dalhausser found a flag, raised it above his head and ran victory laps around the court. Rogers sprinted for his wife and planted a kiss on her lips.

"You really don't realize how cool it is until years and years later," Rogers says. "Your head is a whirl."

Months later, in a quiet moment in a room in South Carolina, Dalhausser would be sitting with his old roommate, Adam Roberts. Roberts wanted to pick the big man's brain on the most momentous moment of his career. He cued up the film of the third set. Dalhausser didn't really want to watch, in fear that it might make him look braggadocios, to re-watch the biggest match of his life. He'd rather talk about Roberts. Roberts insisted. Dalhausser relented. Fine, he'd take a look at the film.

"We're watching it, and Phil runs out of his booth, and he runs out and he's looking up at the sky, looking around, I pause it, saying 'What's going through your mind?'" Roberts recalled. "And he says, 'I remember thinking 'It sure is nice out. They said it wasn't going to be nice out. But it's really nice outside.'

"This is what he's thinking as he's about to start game three of the gold medal match."

Back in the States, as the wait for the 2012 London Olympics began, Gibb and Rosenthal became perpetual finalists, taking second in four of the first six events of the 2009 AVP season before claiming the Manhattan Beach Open title, Gibb's second and Rosenthal's first.

"I think if you ask a lot of volleyball players what the biggest tournament is and they'll say the Manhattan Beach Open," Rosenthal said. "It's the Wimbledon of beach volleyball. It's got a special aura."

In 12 AVP tournaments that year, the two finished outside of the top three only twice, closing the season ranked third on Tour, behind Dalhausser and Rogers and Sean Scott and John Hyden. Then came a truncated 2010 season begat by financial troubles, which preceded a year bereft of the AVP in 2011, the first time since 1976 in which there would be no domestic tour. Many, including Scott, retired. Those who couldn't give the game up fled overseas, which was fine with Rosenthal, who was still single. To him, it just meant "two long summers, tougher competition and more prize money," which is hardly much different than a standard volleyball season.

But it wouldn't be until 2012 that they found their footing again. The year prior was, in Gibb's opinion, "the worst of my career." He and Rosenthal played in 14 FIVB tournaments and didn't win one, and once were eliminated in two matches in Finland. A struggling Gibb called up one of his most trusted confidants, Mike Dodd, and wondered what was wrong. Dodd had won 75 tournaments over the course of his illustrious career, which included five Manhattan Beach Opens and a silver medal in the 1996 Olympics. He knew volleyball. His advice: "Look in a mirror," which reflected a 6-foot-7 man who didn't even tip the scales at 200 pounds. Sure, Gibb was light and lean and quick on his feet, but he was frail. There was no physicality to his game. Beef up, Dodd told him. And so he did, packing on 15 to 20 pounds, discovering his ideal playing weight to be around 215-220.

Dodd's coaching proved prophetic: The next year, Gibb and Rosenthal would climb the ranks of the world tour. They finished second in the third tournament of the year, in Shanghai, bested only by Dalhausser and Rogers in a white-knuckler of a three-setter, 19-21, 24-22, 11-15. A little more than a month later, in Italy, they won, pounding the number one team in the world at the time, Rego and his new partner, Alison Cerutti, 21-13-21-12. Then they did it again in the next tournament, in Switzerland, cruising past Rego and Cerutti in the gold medal match, 21-17-21-17. And in the semifinal that preceded it, Gibb and Rosenthal pasted Dalhausser and Rogers, 21-10, 21-18.

If there were two teams in the world who had a shot at beating Gibb and Rosenthal, it was Rego and Cerutti or Dalhausser and Rogers, and neither had come close.

"There was a different energy," Gibb said. "We were hot. We were pumped."

In the next two international tournaments leading up to the Olympics, Gibb and Rosenthal finished second and third. It had been nearly two months since the two didn't finish a tournament on the podium.

"We were on a big high going into London," Rosenthal said. "It's different being tournament favorites. We felt like we were going to win."

Cerutti and Rego were seeded No. 1 in the London Games; Dalhausser and Rogers two; Gibb and Rosenthal four. Many considered it a three-horse race, with a spot in the finals all but reserved for the United States, which had won three out of four golds since the sport was introduced to the Olympics in 1996. There was no way both teams could be upset prior to the medal rounds.

But forget medals for a moment. In 2012, Phil Dalhausser was just happy to be alive.

Jennifer Corral was a fine volleyball player in her day, the 2001 Volleyball Athlete of the Year and Academic Athlete of the Year in her final season at Ventura College. Her next two years were spent at Tennessee State, where she was twice named the team's MVP. But sometimes a player's indoor skills don't necessarily translate onto the beach. The rules are different, size of the court is smaller, number of players three times less. Not to mention the subtle difference in playing surface, from hardwood to sand of varying consistencies and depths.

It can be too much for an athlete sometimes, even for the best of indoor players. From 2006 through 2010, Corral would play in 25 AVP tournaments and qualify just three times. The AVP was not going to be her career path. But throughout the process, she had grown close with a rather large individual named Phil Dalhausser. Phil also lived in Santa Barbara, and they were mutual friends with Nick Lucena. Lucena decided they'd be a good fit.

"What an idiot," Lucena said, laughing at the memory of the first time Phil met Jen. "What an idiot. He had just broken up with his longtime girlfriend and I was like 'Aw, we're just going to try to get you out there, maybe do a little bit of making out' and sure enough he ended up marrying the first girl he made out with."

Even though Jen's beach career never panned out the way her husband's did, she had still been a longtime athlete, which is an easy way of saying that she had some aches and cuts and bruises here and there. In early summer of 2012, she went in for a standard checkup on her knee, and the doctor, being a friendly, amicable doctor, asked her about her famous, gold-medal-winning husband.

Phil was great! Except…his left arm had been giving him some problems. It went numb sometimes. His forearm and bicep had been unusually tight, particularly during an NVL in Baltimore, where he and Todd lost to an obnoxious kid with a blond mohawk named Casey Patterson and his 7-foot partner, Ryan Doherty. Massages hadn't loosened it up. Neither did stretching or holding his arm above his head. That actually made it worse. Pretty annoying, really. And, wow, you should have seen the size of his arm after they took a flight home from Prague! It was huge!

"Almost double the size of my real arm," Dalhausser says. "I should have taken a picture of it. It was freaky looking."

The doctor had seen this before. He told Dalhausser he likely had a blood clot. He handed him a packet of information, sent him to an imaging center.

"Sure enough," Dalhausser says, "they found two clots. It was the worst timing possible."

Career-wise, yes. Being sidelined for the entire month of June, with the Olympics being held at the end of July, was awful. Health-wise, it's possible the doctor may have found it just in time.

"It could have killed him," Rogers said. "It literally could have killed him."

So for one month, Dalhausser sat on the couch, unable to perform any semblance of physical activity. The blood thinner he was on could have proven just as deadly as the clot.

"Let's say I was chasing after a ball and I hit my head on the pole or something," Dalhausser said. "I could break a blood vessel in my brain and it could be fatal."

Right. No volleyball.

After a month of rest and clearance from the doctor, Dalhausser had regained his health enough to play in three tournaments prior to the Olympics, in Switzerland, Germany and Australia, with mixed results: fourth, ninth, fourth. They showed bursts, here and there, of the gold medal team they were in 2008. They just struggled to sustain it.

"We were playing well, we just ran out of gas," Rogers said. "We weren't as crisp. We weren't in as good of shape as we needed to be. If we turned it on, yeah, we could still beat anyone in the world and we knew that, but it's tough when you have a month break. So we just went in and said 'Let's see how it goes. We're here, let's see how it rolls.' You see how it went down."

What's funny is that London began far better than Beijing. There was no stunning upset to the Latvians, rather the opposite: Dalhausser and Rogers lost just one set during the three pool play matches, making it out of pool play seeded second only to Brazil's Cerutti and Rego. But something just wasn't right. Three matches had taken a toll on Dalhausser's already-sapped capacity for cardio. If the cosmos had indeed all been aligned in Beijing, they were well out of sync in London.

In the first round, they met an enormous Italian pair, 6-foot-5 defender Daniele Lupo and 6-foot-8 blocker Paolo Nicolai.

Down the Americans went in straight sets: 21-17, 21-19.

"I'm not one to make excuses," Dalhausser says. "Winners find a way to win when things aren't perfect and we just didn't find a way to win."

And neither, shockingly, did their compatriots, Rosenthal and Gibb. There was no indication that they had cooled at all from their torrid pre-Olympics run. In their first match of pool play, against South Africa, they allowed a total of 21 points. In their third, against Latvia's top-ranked team, they allowed only 26. Their first round of bracket play, against Russia's Konstantin Semenov and Serguey Prokopyev, was another straight-set win, 21-14, 22-20.

"Jake was playing some of the best volleyball of his life up to that point," said Gibb's good friend John Braunstein, a former AVP player who was in the stands in London. With that in mind, it was easy for one to look ahead in the bracket. Gibb and Rosenthal were scheduled to play Latvia's second team, Martins Plavins and Janis Smedins, a team that Rosenthal says "we'd beat nine out of ten times."

They had, in fact, beaten them five matches in a row. Easy peasy. It should be onto the next one, where they would meet Cerutti and Rego. At one point during the 2012 season, the Brazilians had appeared in six straight title matches. Their prospective clash with Gibb and Rosenthal could have been considered a de facto gold medal match. Until it wasn't.

In the third set with Latvia, after splitting the first two, 19-21, 21-18, Latvia grabbed a 6-2 lead, capitalizing on some uncharacteristically listless play from Gibb, who was blocked twice, had a ball ripped off his block, hit a ball out of bounds. That alone should have been enough for the Latvians to coast in from there, but with the Americans down 9-7, Gibb hit a float serve he has nicknamed the "dancing bear" for its knuckleball movement, and Plavins sprayed the pass. Smedins did well to chase it down and simply keep it in play. Gibb set Rosenthal with an open net. Rosenthal blasted it out of bounds, gift-wrapping a back-breaking point for Latvia.

"Oh, goodness," moaned the color commentator. "That was an unforgivable miss."

On the next point, Rosenthal was dug and Latvia scored in transition and the rest of the match was merely a formality. Latvia won, 15-11, and just like that, in a blink, the United States, a volleyball superpower with two of the top four teams in the world, was out. No medals. No podium. No Star Spangled Banner. Nothing. For the second time in as many tries, Gibb and Rosenthal finished one round shy of vying for an Olympic medal.

"That," Rosenthal said, "is the toughest loss of my career, and I'm sure Jake would say the same thing. You just wanna get out of there and drive straight to the bar."

If it weren't such an incredible achievement, it could almost be viewed as salt in the wound when, less than a month later, the final world rankings were released: Gibb and Rosenthal finished the 2012 season ranked the No. 1 team on the planet. Dalhausser and Rogers were third.

Neither team even competed for an Olympic medal.

"That's just something you never get over because it's not like on the regular Tour when you've got next week to make up for it," Dodd said. "It's a four-year wait and a grind to even qualify after those four years. That match in London, I'll never forget. That was as much as I've ever hurt in sports."

One of the most successful quads American beach volleyball has ever seen had come to an end.

A new one was about to begin.

Casey Patterson doesn't play golf, nor does he really like the sport. But dammit if he was going to miss Tyler Hildebrand's Ryder Cup barbeque on the last weekend of September 2012. It didn't matter if Hildebrand hadn't even invited him. Jake Gibb was going to be there, and Casey had to meet with Gibb.

It began – where else? – with the wives. Hildebrand's wife, Kristin Richards, had grown up best friends with Lexi Brown, who married Patterson in 2005. Well, Kristin told Lexi that, on the weekend of September 29 and 30, the Hildebrands would be having a Ryder Cup barbeque, and wouldn't they like to come?

"Casey all of a sudden hits me up and is like, 'Hey, Kristin told Lexi you were having people over for a BBQ and I know Jake's coming over, is it ok if I come?'" Hildebrand recalled. "And I'm like 'Oh, shit, dude!' Because Jake was very clear, like 'Hey, dude, don't talk to Casey about this.' So I texted Jake and he said 'Yea, dude bring him over.'"

To be clear, Gibb didn't dislike Patterson. But he was also weighing the biggest career decision he had made since he opted to pick up Rosenthal as a partner. The first domino of the new quad had already fallen. It wasn't much of a surprise that Dalhausser had dropped Rogers as a partner – "all good things," Dalhausser says, "come to an end." When Rosenthal got the call from perhaps the greatest blocker alive that he wanted to partner up, it was an offer no sane volleyball player could decline. Which left Gibb without a partner, though certainly not without options.

The safe route was Lucena. He was proven. The 2008 AVP Defensive Player of the Year, Lucena had won domestically three times – the first with Dalhausser in 2005 in Austin – and made an admirable run at the 2012 Olympics with Matt Fuerbringer.

The risky route was Patterson, who was 6-foot-6 but played the same side as Gibb and had only been playing defense for one year, behind Ryan Doherty's 7-foot block. There was also the matter that, as a player, Gibb was not a huge fan of Patterson.

In August of 2015, Gibb would pen this in the Players' Tribune, an online platform for athletes to publish their own work: "Another thing about Casey: I didn't really like him at first. Casey's reputation preceded him. He was this young cocky guy making noise at tournaments. He was a great indoor college player who was coming up through the ranks in beach. There was no doubt about his skill level, but he was also known for ... how do you put it? Being loud. I mean loud in every sense of the word. Dancing between plays. Talking trash (he's probably the best trash talker on the AVP Tour). Going right back at hecklers in the crowd. Flaunting that haircut, the yellow Mohawk. He's a fan favorite, for sure, but if he's playing against your team, he gets under your skin. At first I looked at this kid and I was like, What have you done yet? I only saw the trash-talking Mohawk guy."

It's funny, then, what happened next: Patterson crashed the Ryder Cup barbeque. He and Gibb talked in Hildebrand's jacuzzi. A new partnership was formed.

"Jake was willing to take a massive risk on his coach and his partner," Hildebrand said. "I think the safe bet was Nick and he took a risk with Casey. Everybody knows Casey as this guy who's like 'Nobody gave me a chance, I'm going to prove everybody wrong, screw the world.' A lot of people are like 'You're pretty good, but the World Tour is different.' But that's what Jake needed – a young, talented, hungry guy. Casey was so ready to prove to everybody that he could do it."

Oh, was he ready all right.

In May of 2013, they won their second tournament together, an FIVB Grand Slam in China. They didn't even lose a match.

"I'm like 'Shit, man, is this how it goes?'" Hildebrand, the duo's coach, recalled. "People don't understand that the World Tour is such a joke. It's like golf. Everyone can win. Legitimately 15 to 18 teams can win a Grand Slam. It's so gnarly."

For most teams, no, no that's not how it goes. In nine tournaments on the FIVB Tour prior to partnering up with Gibb, Patterson had only finished better than 17th twice. He had never even made the quarterfinals.

With Gibb, everything would change. And fast.

AVP MANHATTAN BEACH

"You're in the Valhalla, the heaven for the Gods."

Tyler Hildebrand still doesn't know why he did it. In all of the wins during which he had coached Casey Patterson and Jake Gibb – in Shanghai and St. Petersburg, in Huntington Beach and New York, in New Orleans and Atlantic City and Salt Lake City, among half a dozen others – he had never once run onto the court and celebrated.

"It's their moment," the coach said. "Not mine."

He stays in the coach's box. He'll wait until Patterson and Gibb have finished their interviews and kissed their wives and shaken the hands of those whose hands need shaking. Then, and only then, will he celebrate with his boys. But July 17, 2016, in Manhattan Beach was just…different.

More than 100,000 fans made their way to Manhattan Beach that weekend for the 57th Manhattan Beach Open, and they witnessed one of the best finals in its storied history: Tri Bourne, the star in the making, the future face of American beach volleyball, and John Hyden, the grizzled vet and winner of two Manhattan Beach Opens; vs. Jake Gibb, the three-time Olympian and two-time Manhattan winner and Casey Patterson, the trash-talking, mohawk-rocking, voluble first-time Olympian who had lost his only Manhattan final appearance, in 2012, to Hyden and Sean Scott.

It was 14-13 in the third set. Match point. Bourne served Gibb. A mistake. Bourne and Hyden miscommunicated, both taking the line, leaving an enormous void of open court for Gibb, who pounded it away easily. Gibb shimmied, a rare show of panache for the player many liken to the NBA's Tim Duncan, the stoic, fundamental personification of San Antonio Spurs hoops.

14-14.

Gibb served down Bourne's line and they ran a dive, with Gibb taking the angle late and Patterson filling line behind him. Bourne took the bait, hitting a high line shot, exactly what Patterson wanted. He dug it and ripped Gibb's set down the middle.

15-14.

It was Patterson and Gibb's match to win now, but would history sneak up on them, as it had in Manhattan Beach throughout their entire partnership? All told, the four years leading up to that moment had been one of the most successful partnerships in recent AVP history. They had won 11 tournaments in 25 tries. Patterson even called his wife, Lexi, and asked her if this was real life, and he asked Gibb if it was really always this easy, to which Gibb responded: "Dude, this is unreal to me, too."

But there was one tournament that eluded their grasp: The Manhattan Beach Open. In 2015, they had been knocked out in the quarterfinals by the Crabb brothers, Taylor and Trevor, in what Gibb says is one of the top 10 matches he has ever played in, a 31-29, 17-21, 14-16 thriller. The year before had no such theatrics. They took seventh. It was the only tournament that year that they did not make the finals. In 2013, they had fallen victim to Phil Dalhausser and Sean Rosenthal in the semifinals.

In the 25 tournaments that Gibb and Patterson had played together, there had been only four instances in which they did not make the semifinals. Three of them occurred in Manhattan Beach.

"To me it would have been kind of a travesty, for the body of work that they put in on the AVP Tour, just domination and winning tournaments, to not be together forever on the pier," Hildebrand said. "It would have been a travesty. We put that tournament on a pedestal."

With good reason.

Ask any American beach volleyball player what the biggest tournament of the year is, and the answer will unanimously be Manhattan Beach. The first Manhattan Beach Open was held in 1960, and it hasn't missed a year since. It has become a divinity on the AVP schedule. You can miss Seattle or New York City or even Chicago. You cannot miss Manhattan.

"If you're playing in the United States, for sure, Manhattan is number one," Patterson said. "That's the one when you're 50, you can go to the pier and show your kids that you won. Only the legends have won. You're in the legends club. You're in the Valhalla, the heaven for the Gods."

The Gods.

They go by Smith and Stoklos and Hovland and Dodd. They go by Von Hagen and O'Hara and Bright and Lang. And just like the Gods, the winners of the Manhattan Beach Open will be immortal in the beach volleyball Mount Zion that is Manhattan Beach, California.

"I think you start with the history and tradition of the tournament," Mike Dodd, winner of five Manhattan Beach Opens, said. "It has been, since it ever started, the tournament that has the biggest crowd, the best setup, the best court, the nicest everything. Even in the 1960s, anyone who played beach volleyball, that was your Olympics, that was your pinnacle, to win a Manhattan Open. It was always the toughest tournament with the biggest field and all the tradition and all those factors. The Manhattan was our Olympics. The Olympics are the Olympics and they're something that nothing can really compare to but the Manhattan Open just keeps going on."

Dodd knows as well as any. He won his first Manhattan Beach Open in 1982 with Tim Hovland, when he was just 25 years old and Hovland 23. And then they won the next, in 1983, and the next, and the next, and even one more after that, five straight, a record that stands to this day.

"We called ourselves the big game hunters because we'd win Manhattan, Hermosa, the Cuervos," Hovland said. "We'd give them the Rhode Islands, Phoenixes, those things."

He hasn't lost his wit, Hov. He became a sexagenarian not too long ago. He's aged well. No mistaking that. Carved out a nice little niche in real estate. Married. Kids. Still signing autographs and taking pictures. A living legend.

Truth be told, Hovland could have gone pro in whatever sport he chose to pursue. As a standout at Westchester High School, Hovland was named to the All-City teams for basketball, football and volleyball, and he had no shortage of offers from colleges. He had his pick of schools, playing his pick of sport. Could have played football, basketball or volleyball wherever he so chose. At the end of the day, he opted for volleyball at USC, a decision he confirmed when, upon returning from a trip to Brazil with the junior national team, "I saw Ronnie Lott [a safety on the football team], hit this guy into fucking next week and I just said 'You know what? I'm just going to play volleyball,'" he recalled. "It sure seems like there's a bunch more chicks and you don't have to break your god damn – get broken in half out here. That's when I decided to stay with volleyball."

At the time, it was viewed as an odd choice. This was an age before concussion awareness was in vogue. Football was king. Exceptional athletes didn't choose non-contact sports in '70s America, and Hovland was, make no mistake, an exceptional athlete, named the Southern California High School Athlete of the Year in 1978. His main competition? Lott, who in 1981 would become a first-round draft pick for the San Francisco 49ers and in 2000 be named to the Pro Football Hall of Fame.

"Ronnie is still pissed to this day," Hovland said of being named the High School Athlete of the Year over Lott. "We went to SC together, and I wouldn't let him forget it, and now I see him all the time because his daughter plays volleyball, and he's still mad about it."

160

With its pair of heralded recruits, USC thrived. Lott led the football team to a national championship in 1978 and a pair of Rose Bowls in 1979 and '80. Hovland took the volleyball team to three national championship berths, toppling Kiraly and the mighty Bruins in 1980.

The NFL called for Lott. Professional indoor teams in Italy called for Hovland. Both lives seemed idyllic.

"I would go to Italy, make a couple hundred thousand over there, then I would come over here," Hovland said.

It was the exact same routine that a young man named Mike Dodd had been doing.

Dodd was not named the Southern California High School Athlete of the Year. In fact, the thin and underdeveloped kid out of Mira Costa High School didn't have a single scholarship offer. Not for volleyball. Not for basketball. Not for anything. It was nothing more than dumb luck, a stroke of providence, that Dodd's coach at Mira Costa was a friend of Tim Fezie, who was the basketball coach at San Diego State. The Aztecs, it so happened, had an extra scholarship and could use a guard.

Dodd was on the team.

He rode the bench during his freshman season and saw minimal time as a sophomore. But in his junior season, after filling out and maturing as an athlete, Dodd's 14 points per game ranked second on the team. He led the Aztecs to a 19-9 record, tied for first in the Pacific Coast Athletic Conference.

The next year, he averaged 12 points per game, falling just 82 shy of 1,000 for his career, enough to be drafted in the eighth round by the San Diego Clippers.

He was cut in three days.

Three days. That was it. A lifetime goal had been realized. A lifetime goal had been extinguished. Dodd was not going to be an NBA player.

What now?

He had two options: Play basketball overseas in Germany, where he had been offered a contract. Or play a fifth year at San Diego State – for the volleyball team.

"It just seemed like I had really given basketball my all and after I got cut by the Clippers I just really felt that I needed to get back to volleyball and see how far I could go in that sport," Dodd said. "It was just one of those decisions."

In his lone collegiate year playing indoor volleyball, he impressed enough to get an invite to train with the United States National Team, right alongside UCLA's stars Karch Kiraly and Sinjin Smith and USC's pride, Hovland.

After practices, Kiraly and Smith would head to the beach for a practice on the sand, and they needed a team to train against. Thus was born the team that would become known as Hovvy-Dodd.

"The whole beach thing just grew and grew and grew," Dodd said. "Both Tim Hovland and myself had a really interesting lifestyle. Both of us left the national team to play professionally indoors in Italy and so we would play indoor professional volleyball for these club teams and then we would come home and play professional beach volleyball. After playing four or five years in Italy the beach had grown, adding enough stops that we could play full time."

In 1986, beach volleyball had become so lucrative that "I was almost losing money," Dodd told the LA Times, "by going to Italy."

So he and Hovland both quit traveling overseas, choosing instead to remain in Southern California, professional beach volleyball players both, living a life that, just five years earlier, would have been considered at best a pipe dream, if not a fairy tale altogether.

"We were groundbreakers," Hovland said. "We were doing whatever the hell we wanted to do, but we were in the best shape of anybody. We'd play, we'd work out, we'd party hard. Yeah, it was hard living, but it was fun. It was goddamn fun, I'll tell you that."

Every morning at 10 a.m., Hovland and Dodd would set up the lines at their court on Manhattan Beach's Marine Street, winning every match until 2 p.m. They'd grab some lunch, rest, return, win some more until 5 and then barbeque and drink and go out on the town. Then they'd do it again.

"That was tip-tops, man," Hovland said. "Tip-tops."

A few miles north, Smith and Stoklos would do much of the same, and the reps paid off in equal measure for both.

In 1986, of the 25 tournaments, just one was not won by either Hovvy-Dodd or Smith-Stoklos. The lone exception: The Jose Cuervo Santa Cruz Open, which was won by Scott Ayakatubby and Brent Frohoff. Hovvy-Dodd finished second; Smith-Stoklos third. Nine times the two powers met in the finals, and in a five-tournament stretch from August 23-September 21, no other team made the finals. It was five consecutive bouts of Hovvy-Dodd vs. Smith-Stoklos.

"It's kinda like the old Boston Celtics and Los Angeles Lakers," Hovland said of the rivalry. "You're going to get through these other guys. They might get you once in a while, but very rarely. And when they did, you go through the loser's bracket, and you're only going to get better and better, because you're playing more games and you're not going to get tired. So we just had more determination. We worked harder. That's the damn truth."

It showed, namely in their performances at the Manhattan Beach Open, with a record five consecutive victories that still stands today. Sure, everyone else could have the Phoenixes or Santa Barbaras. They'd be more than happy to continue claiming Manhattan.

"In Santa Barbara, in the finals, there was hardly anyone at all, maybe 500 people," Larry Rundle told the Los Angeles Times in 1989. "But at Manhattan, I remember my dad telling me later: 'They were three-deep all the way around the pier. *Three-deep!*'"

Most players didn't mark their calendars when the AVP stopped by Dallas, but they would for Manhattan Beach. Hovland did when he was 12 years old. He rode his bike to watch Ron Von Hagen, that titan whose legend has reached Paul Bunyan-like status. The Babe Ruth of

Beach Volleyball – that's what Von Hagen has been dubbed. He didn't even pick up a ball until he was a senior at UCLA, and, as his fawning bio in the CBVA Hall of Fame suggests, "Once he found the sport he loved, Von Hagen attacked it was a single-minded devotion that hasn't been seen since."

His beach career spanned 16 years, in which he played in 122 tournaments and won more than half. Five of those victories came at Manhattan Beach, and to choose which is the most epic is tantamount to choosing your favorite child.

How about 1967? When Manhattan Beach hadn't yet barred alcohol from its beaches, beauty contests were in vogue, fights were customary. In the finals, as expected, were Von Hagen and Ron Lang – The Ronnies, as they were called. Not so expected were their opponents: Bill Leeka and Bob Vogelsang.

Leeka had been an All-American football player at UCLA. He weighed 260 pounds and was everything you wouldn't imagine a beach volleyball player to be. Vogelsang had only played in six open tournaments and was known far more for his mouth than his spike. Which didn't help matters when Vogelsang and Leeka opted to drink beer throughout the tournament. By the time of the finals, Vogelsang and Leeka were, well – they were enjoying themselves. They stalled. They played to the crowd. They talked trash. Von Hagen walked under the net, and when everything suggested a fight was about to break out, Leeka planted a kiss on Von Hagen's cheek, turned and flexed to the crowd, and promptly flipped Von Hagen the bird.

The crowd loved it, erupting into chants for Leeka. They rained beer cans onto the court. Someone threw a bottle of wine. Lang chucked it back. More beer cans followed. It was a circus, and Leeka was the ringleader. But that's the thing about the circus: It's only an act. Von Hagen and Lang were no act. Through beer and wine and kisses and flexing, they won their second consecutive Manhattan Beach Open.

Their attempt for a third would be equally as wild.

The rules for beach volleyball in 1968 were not made for television. Or the natural limitations of daylight. With side out scoring, where you could only score a point if you were the serving team, there was no telling how long a match could take. Could be 30 minutes. Could be three hours. There was no certain way of knowing.

And so it was, when Henry Bergman and Larry Rundle beat Von Hagen and Lang in the first set of the final, forcing what's known as a double-final, since that had been Von Hagen and Lang's first loss in a double-elimination tournament, in which a team has to lose twice in order to be knocked out, the clock read 7:30 p.m.

"The four of us, with our combination of skills, were just able to keep it going until the sun went down, and that's exactly what happened," Rundle told the LA Times. "Nobody missed passes, nobody overset and nobody could dig anybody, and the crowd would just explode when somebody finally made a point. People just didn't leave the beach. There was this incredible match going on and they had to find out who was going to win."

Lang and Von Hagen jumped out to an 8-3 lead, but there was a problem: Lang couldn't see a thing. As legend tells it, a number of fans drove their cars onto the beach and turned their lights on, though they only briefly illuminated the court. You still couldn't see anything more than a few feet over the net. Rundle had one of the best skyball serves on tour, difficult to pass even when the players could see the entire flight of the ball.

How could they pass it if they couldn't see it?

The answer: They couldn't. Twice the ball hit the sand without Lang or Von Hagen managing to touch it, and Rundle aced his way to one of 13 open wins and a Manhattan Beach Open title.

"It finally ended when Lang couldn't see the ball anymore in the last game to 15 and we ran through them," said Rundle, who led the indoor American Olympic team to one of its greatest upsets, a five-setter over Russia, that same year. "I said a few years ago at the Manhattan Open champions dinner that tournament should have been called a draw. I still feel that way."

"That was the most famous beach volleyball match of all-time," said Chris Marlowe, who won the event in 1976 and 1977, to the LA Times. "And Manhattan was the biggest. It was always the biggest tournament of the summer."

The legend continued to build, until on August 8, 1996, the biggest tournament became even bigger. Steve Barnes, then the mayor of Manhattan Beach, dedicated a tribute to the winners of the Manhattan Beach Open: The names of the champions would now be immortalized in bronze, volleyball-shaped plaques on the Manhattan Beach Pier's Beach Volleyball Walk of Fame.

"Part of it is just the mystique. Manhattan is the only tournament I know of that puts your name in bronze and puts you on the pier of one of the most famous piers in the world," said Jon Mesko, who has played in 12 Manhattan Beach Opens and made a point to get married on the weekend of his first, in 2004. "No other tournament in the world does that. I think it's that simple little thing combined with the location and the mystique."

It's one of Dodd's favorite past-times, to walk along the Pier, smelling the salt of the Pacific, feeling the cool ocean breeze on his face, looking down to read his name once, twice, thrice, then again, and again.

"I can honestly say it never gets old," Dodd said. "Not just to see my name and my partner Tim Hovland's name, but to see everybody's name – the old players and the new players. Certainly beach volleyball has had its ups and downs, but the soul of the game will always be there."

It is why Jake Gibb, he of three Olympic Games and 33-and-counting victories, has exactly two items in his household that would reflect what he did for a living. The first is a panorama of the 1976 Manhattan Beach Open, because "I wanted a picture of 'Where the Manhattan Beach Open was when I was born,'" he said.

The second is a picture of the 2005 Manhattan Beach Open finals, when Gibb and Stein Metzger would pound Phil Dalhausser and Nick Lucena 21-19, 21-10, cementing – literally – Gibb's status as a Manhattan Beach Open champion.

"There's nothing like it," Gibb said. "It's one of those where you get the legends to come out and watch your matches and there's more pressure on it, you're a little more nervous. I've had a funny ride with Manhattan where I've either had the worst finish of the year but then I've won it three times."

The legends are still there, every year. Stoklos and Smith sit next to their once-bitter rivals, Hovland and Dodd. Decades have passed since their first wins on beach volleyball's biggest stage, though it doesn't much matter. Time only seems to add to their myth, same as it has with Von Hagen and Lang.

"This is our backyard. This is where we live. You gotta win your home game, plus you have all your girlfriends and friends. You gotta win Manhattan. You could be a great player, but if you haven't won Manhattan, you haven't lived yet," Hovland said. "Once you win, you're in the club. You've won Wimbledon. It's the big one. If you don't win it, you can't be one of the best. Randy, Sinjin, Dodd – all those people at Manhattan remember us more than they know these people now!

"I took more pictures and signed more autographs [at the 2017 Manhattan Beach Open]. It's kind of funny. These people are like 'Hey! I met my wife at the Manhattan Beach Open in 1983, do you remember that one?' And it's like 'No, I don't, I was playing.' It's pretty funny. A lot of old memories there, that's for damn sure."

Leading 15-14 in the third set of the 2016 Manhattan Beach Open, Gibb served Bourne again. Again, they ran a dive. And again, Bourne took the bait, rolling a line shot that Patterson easily dug. The crowd was on its feet, having witnessed 67 minutes of the most electrifying championship match of the year. And when Patterson put it away on a hard angle swing, it went bonkers. Patterson immediately sprinted into the stands.

Did that really just happen?

Did I really just win the Manhattan Beach Open?

Bourne and Hyden walked in circles, heads down. Hyden clasped his hands as one would in a prayer, putting them to his mouth in disbelief. And then you see it: a 32-year-old man sprinting onto the court, something he had never before done, looking for someone, anyone, to hug, the beach volleyball version of Jim Valvano stumbling onto the court after N.C. State won the 1983 college basketball National Championship. Hildebrand finds Gibb. He lifts him off his feet, 6-foot-7 be damned.

"You don't understand how special it is until you do it," Hildebrand said. "Something happens when you win. You hear about the U.S. Open or Augusta or Wimbledon or whatever, just something changes when you win it and you're like 'Whoa.' To me that was the crowning moment of their partnership. It was a lot more fun to talk about than the Olympics."

AVP CHICAGO

"If I had to do it again, I wouldn't change it for the world"

"You've gotta be fucking kidding me."

Chris Luers couldn't believe it. Still can't. He had done everything – *everything* – right. He had traveled to all the tournaments. He had played with the same partner, 27-year-old Jon Drake. They had played top-tier ball against top-tier opponents.

And in the final event of the year, the AVP Championships in Chicago, they were nudged out of the coveted automatic main draw seeding, shoved right back into the qualifier – their seventh qualifier of the year.

Then again, wasn't that just how this season was going, anyhow?

Their litany of heartbreaks began in the very first tournament, in New Orleans. They had been knocked out in the second round by Chase Frishman and Mike Brunsting, traveling 800 miles just to play two matches with weather-truncated games to 11.

Drake's budget for the season was nearly blown right then.

He and Luers had gone in hoping for the best, expecting the worst. They even bought their return flights to Ohio for Thursday, the night of the qualifier. They assumed they wouldn't make main draw. If they made it, they'd just invest the winnings in a new plane ticket.

But torrential downpour had pushed the start of play back so far that by the time Luers and Drake played their second-round match against Frishman and Brunsting, "it was in total darkness," Luers said. They had missed their flights before the first serve.

After losing a match that lasted all of 18 minutes, they had to buy $400 one-way tickets back to Cincinnati, wet, pissed, despondent.

"New Orleans was just shitty," Drake said.

A month later, they played some of the best ball of their lives in the Huntington Beach Open – and still lost in the third round. Seattle, a month after that, was a first-round knockout. New York in mid-July? Dismissed by the McKibbins, Riley and Maddison, in the final qualifying round.

Manhattan Beach was the exception. They had earned an automatic main draw bid by winning their region in the AVP Next developmental series, and even then, Drake knew it wasn't the same. They had beaten up on inferior opponents on a coast where beach volleyball is an afterthought to afterthoughts.

Chicago, the AVP Championship, was their shot at making a main draw by way of qualifier or – even better – by direct seeding. It would be legitimate – no loopholes, no side door. While they hadn't made it through a qualifier in their two years trying together, they had placed well enough in the qualifying tournaments to build up their AVP points, which improves seeding in the qualifiers. With Chicago being the final event, featuring a 24-team main draw, as opposed to the standard 16, they might just be directly in.

"Chris was looking at it, and he said 'You know, we have a shot,'" Drake said. And Luers was right: They would have been the 20th and final automatic main draw team. Until they weren't. Dan Buehring and Matthew McCarthy, a pair of midwest players who had played one combined event that year, signed up. McCarthy's points from the previous year had been frozen – not lost, as they typically would be when a player doesn't play in events – because of an injury. And just like that, Drake and Luers were back in the qualifier.

"We got real salty," Drake said. "We were a little annoyed but Chris was like 'Being handed a main draw ticket is pretty awesome. But let me tell you, there's no better feeling when that last ball drops and you get into the main draw. Let's earn this one.' He always says 'If you want to prove that you're main draw, you have to beat the teams in the qualifier.'"

And that's exactly what they did.

The first match was a comfortable 21-14, 21-14 victory, and they survived a grueling three-setter in the second. By the time they started their third and final match, most of the other players were finished. A crowd formed. Drake had friends and family in town. So did Luers. A perfect setting for a perfect breakthrough. They won game one, 21-16, and Luers couldn't help but get excited.

"We are so close," he told Drake. "Trust me, this is going to be awesome."

And when leading 22-21 in the second set, match point, *qualifying point*, Luers made a dig and took his quick set out of the middle and knuckled one towards the line, his signature shot, and down it went. Alas, after two years of trying – and failing – to qualify on the AVP Tour, they had done it: These two Ohioans, beach volleyball misfits if there ever were any, had qualified for a main draw.

"It was probably the most fun I've ever had in beach volleyball," Luers said. "Just bringing Jon along and letting him see what it's like to grind and battle for two straight years and to finally make it through. I think that's the joy – if I had to do it again I wouldn't trade it for the world right there."

"That was for sure the best feeling I've ever had, of any match I've ever won," Drake said. "That win was really, really awesome. Just playing all season, earning that one seed, and we took advantage of it, making it all the way through. You just finally got the accomplishment, we finally made our trip worth it, we finally got what we were striving for. That's what it's all about, all the traveling time, the hotel, taking off work, getting out there and doing what we were wanting to do all season at the very end, it just made the whole season worth it."

It was a momentous victory for Drake and Luers. But it was also an indelible moment for every beach volleyball player living outside of California. Drake and Luers, Ohioans both, had sent a message: It can be done. You can live in Ohio, or Virginia, or New Jersey, or New York, and you can be a professional beach volleyball player.

Hell, you can even live in Minnesota.

On January 26, 2016, Casey Patterson was shoveling. It was a fairly routine chore that time of year for the most recognizable face on the AVP Tour. Nearly 2,000 miles away in Minnesota, another duo, Tim and Brian Bomgren, had been doing much of the same.

Though here it may be important to note one slight difference: The Bomgrens had been shoveling snow. Nineteen inches of the stuff. So no, they did not train on January 26, as Patterson did, when he was shoveling the sand on his court in Huntington Beach to smooth it out. Didn't train on the day before that. Skipped the day before that one, too. It's tough to play beach volleyball when there is a blanket of snow covering your court.

"There are probably guys out in California training right now," Tim said. "Yeah, that's not us."

He was correct. There were plenty of players training in California. Almost all of them, really. There were not any players training in Minnesota. And he's ok with that. Minnesota is home. Where it's always been. And more than likely where it's always going to be. Which makes the Bomgren team something of a volleyball unicorn.

It's a peculiar situation for a beach volleyball team, not to mention one of the top duos in the country. Peruse the AVP rankings and you will find that 41 of the top 50 players from the 2016 season are listed as

California natives. Several who aren't – take Robbie Page and Stafford Slick, for example – have since relocated.

The Bomgrens have not. They're Minnesotans born and raised, as evidenced by their love for the Minnesota Vikings and an apparent immunity to cold weather.

"I can remember a number of times, we're chomping at the bit to see a ball in the sand, and we're out there in pants and long sleeves and sand socks – not because the sand is hot, but because it's cold," Brian, the defender and elder of the two, said. "And when the ball bounces off the court it'll go into the snow. That's early season practice for us."

It's fair to wonder: How exactly is a team from Minnesota, who sometimes can't begin training until late April or even early May, the month the AVP begins its season most years, making its ascent as one of the best in beach volleyball?

The answer could be as simple as the seven-letter name they share.

"Because they're brothers, their team chemistry – you can't beat that," said Chris McDonald, who played the Bomgrens in the New Orleans qualifier in 2015. "They just have this unbelievable connection. It's almost like when twins finish each other's sentences."

Or sets. McDonald should know. The Bomgrens pasted him and his partner, Drew Pitlik, 21-15, 21-13, in the 2015 New Orleans qualifier to move onto the next round, and they would win their next two qualifying matches, make main draw, and finish third, their best finish on the AVP Tour. No team came within three points of the Minnesotans in the qualifier, and the only duos to beat them in the main draw both wound up in the finals – Patterson and Jake Gibb, and Phil Dalhausser and Sean Rosenthal, four eventual Olympians.

"Was it a surprise?" Tim said of the 2015 season-opening finish. "Maybe we made it a little farther than we thought but certainly our expectations are up there."

Added Brian: "We both analyze the game and know that we might not win this 50 percent of the time, or even 20 percent of the time, but we're able to see what we do well and how we could win."

It's that same strategy, in fact, that led them to one of their first career main draw victories on the AVP Tour, over Dalhausser and Rosenthal in Santa Barbara 2013, a year after both competed in the London Olympics.

"Mentally, looking at that match, they would beat us nine times out of ten," Brian said. "But we knew they haven't seen us play, and we knew if we do A, B and C, and do them really well, we could win. We weren't shell shocked. We look at matches strategically."

It is nothing shy of astounding to most players the Bomgrens compete against that they are doing this while training in a state that, as Tim readily admitted, "is not exactly the Mecca of beach volleyball."

"They're not taking the easy road by being in Minnesota," said Ed Ratledge, a California native who had played the Bomgrens five times through 2016. "I'm sure that they have a competitive training group, but Phil Dalhausser isn't rolling through Minnesota to train."

Despite the fact that Brian now has a beach volleyball court in his backyard – a project he undertook in the summer of 2015 – their location is nearly unanimously viewed as a burden. Except for two people: Tim and Brian Bomgren.

"I would say it's mandatory to live in California," said Matt Olson, a two-time AVP champion who was raised in San Diego. "But I can't say mandatory because of the Bomgrens. I don't know what their deal is. Those guys are grinding and working on the things they need to work on. If we didn't know those guys existed, I would say it's mandatory."

There are exceptions to every rule, and the Bomgrens are certainly the exception for this one. The longer, snow-induced off-season, Tim said, provides a longer rest period, both mentally and physically. While injuries hobble or nag nearly every AVP main draw player each season, the Bomgrens remain fully healthy, with no signs of burnout. They also don't necessarily believe they need an extra four or five months over the off-season to train. They're more than content putting in hours at Anytime Fitness before work until the weather warms up and they're able to get some touches on the ball.

"Because Brian and I are such competitors and athletes, we're so focused when the season starts," Tim said.

And they are athletes indeed. They played "pretty much every sport there is to play" growing up, mostly basketball, baseball and golf, which Brian played for Bethel University, a small, Christian school in Arden Hills, Minnesota. It wasn't until Brian played some indoor volleyball with a couple college buddies that the two seriously dove into the sport.

After graduating from Bethel, Brian, as older brothers are wont to do, told Tim that they would be playing together from there on out. It didn't take long for them to realize that all of those football games and basketball tournaments, golf matches and baseball doubleheaders had molded them into the ideal athletes for beach volleyball.

"A well-rounded athlete is much more rewarded because you have to do everything," Brian said. "It's not like football where you can be good at just one thing and that's going to work."

Their athleticism is most evident on the defensive end of the game. Despite standing 6-foot-4 – undersized for a blocker; for comparison's sake, Gibb is 6-foot-7, Dalhausser 6-foot-9 – in 2015 Tim finished fifth on the AVP in blocks (92) and Brian fifth in digs (282).

"They touched every ball," said Tom Kohler, who lost to the Bomgrens in Manhattan Beach in 2015. "There were no easy points in the match against them. I don't know what they do but they always seemed like they were on the same page."

That's how it goes with most aspects of volleyball for the Bomgrens, including the location in which they want to play it. They are asked dozens of times each year if they are going to move to California. And they will respond dozens of times with a variation of the same answer: It's not happening.

"Volleyball is a huge plus to be able to compete, but I have higher priorities in my life," Brian said. He's a successful quantitative portfolio manager, married with two kids. Tim, a technical support engineer for a software company, is married with a kid of his own. They go to work, hang out with their families, play volleyball when they can. That's life. And they're quite enamored with it.

As for volleyball? It's "a hobby that we spend a lot of time doing," Tim said.

And doing, it's key to note, together. They've had offers for partnerships outside of the family, of course. Tim especially. Blockers are hard enough to find. But left-handed blockers who can dig off the net, side out consistently, set well and make plays only the exceptionally gifted can make?

Yes, Tim is a rarity.

"Just let me know," Stafford Slick likes to joke, "when you're ready to play defense."

They'd make a fair team, Bomgren and Slick, not only for the fact that they're two magnificent athletes, and Slick's massive, 6-foot-8 block and exceptional setting would be a perfect complement to Bomgren's athleticism and ability to side out in transition, but because they both call the same state home.

Slick, three years Tim's senior, was born in Andover, Minnesota, roughly 40 miles from the Bomgrens' home in Woodbury. And, just like those Bomgrens, he grew up playing everything but volleyball, all basketball and baseball, a good enough pitcher to be named captain, sizable enough on the basketball court to be a formidable presence inside. The issue with his size, though, was that it was straight up and down, not out.

"I didn't weigh anything," he said, laughing. His fastballs didn't pack much heat and, thin as he was, he wasn't much of a bruiser on the hardwood.

"I never really had any intention to play basketball or baseball," he said. "I was kinda fried by the time I got done high school."

He wasn't fried with all sports, just the two he had grown up on and subsequently got burned out of. It was at a freshman orientation at the University of Minnesota, when a billion clubs were handing out a billion informational cards, that Slick was introduced to volleyball. His girlfriend, Julie, who would later become his wife, had played in high school and went on to compete for Michigan Tech. When he thought about it, volleyball had everything he wanted in a sport.

"It had everything I liked about basketball and none of the things I didn't like," he said. "I was the center but I got tossed around because I was too light. I could just jump high like I was dunking and I could take all that physicality and channel that sort of aggression not against a player but against an inanimate object."

In his second year with the club team, they made it to nationals, "and it was just non-stop volleyball courts," Slick recalled. "I was in heaven."

He was also, talent-wise, in over his head. For there, too, was Arizona, the best club team in the country. But what he saw wasn't discouraging, rather just the opposite. What Slick saw was a group of talented individuals who were high caliber, to be sure, but "they didn't jump any higher," Slick said. "I knew I could play at that level, I just needed more experience."

In 2009, after finishing up his masters in educational psychology, Slick tried out for the USA Volleyball High Performance team, which is essentially an adult developmental program that trains for a few weeks in Hermosa Beach every summer, a pipeline to uncover and groom the next generation of beach volleyball talent. Which is a bit amusing, given the fact that Slick had never heard of men by the names of Phil Dalhausser or Todd Rogers, the 2008 gold medalists and No. 1 ranked team in the world.

"Just crushing people on the world tour," Slick said. "And I had no idea."

He would leave the team as confused as he entered, though in vastly different manners. Slick had received the equivalent of Beach Volleyball 101, with real coaching and real strategy, where he began to develop real skills, not just the self-taught kind. He was smitten. And torn. Torn between the perpetual reckoning beach volleyball players inevitably must confront: the beach, or what many refer to as the "real world," the one east of California's famed Pacific Coast Highway.

"I went back to Minnesota, played a few tournaments, but I kept thinking about Hermosa and the feedback that I got and what I wanted to do with my life," Slick said. "It was that weird phase in my life where it's like 'What do I want to do with my life?' My job interviews were coming to fruition so it was a weird little time lapse for me where I didn't know what my next move was going to be."

At the end of the summer, he had his answer. At the AVP's final stop of the season, in Chicago during the last weekend of August, Slick entered the qualifier with Ryan Vander Veen. They lost in the second round to a team that would eventually make it to the main draw. Slick knew he could play with those guys, that he could beat those guys, that main draw was his for the taking, that this life on the beach was a genuine possibility.

"It was one of those things where you kind of do it or don't," Slick said. "I made that decision to go for it."

He went home, packed two suitcases, bought a one-way ticket on Northwest Airlines and set out for Hermosa Beach. A new life. A beach life.

"I did a lot of soul searching and tried to convince myself that I was making an intelligent decision," Slick said. "But it was a low risk situation. If I went and it didn't work I could always come back to Minnesota."

The safety net of home wouldn't be necessary. Slick wouldn't let it. He took a job at a college planning company where he worked 50 hours a week. He kept fit by doing P90X in his apartment, and "any daylight hours I wasn't working, I was that guy playing volleyball by himself, serving to different spots on the court, running up and blocking, just a total goofball," he recalled. "It was what I needed to do in order to make it work."

He didn't have a car so he'd bike to the beach. He worked remote, sometimes taking calls before or after practice. He hauled groceries on his bike, which got a bit tedious but it was what he needed to do.

People noticed. A man named Dain Blanton, a gold medalist in the 2000 Olympics, noticed, picking up Slick for the AVP's stop in Hermosa Beach in 2010, Slick's first main draw. He was a 6-foot-8 deer in the headlights. He reveled in the fact that he could get free massages, unlimited massages. Free Oakley's.

And was that Rogers and Dalhausser? Sitting right next to him? Chatting about life and volleyball?

How sweet is that?

"It's like 'Holy shit! These are the guys!'" Slick recalled, laughing. Within three years, Slick was one of those guys. In 2013, when the AVP held its first full season under new owner Donald Sun, Slick was picked up by Casey Jennings, who had narrowly missed the 2012 Olympic Games. They claimed a seventh in their first tournament, and two events later, Slick was partnered with a brash, swaggering, 6-foot dynamo named Adrian Carambula, an Italian with a towering serve and a homegrown, streetball style of play. Together, they logged four straight top-fives, and Slick knew, "Ok, I fucking belong here now," he said. "I was in it."

In it enough that by 2015 he was picked up by Rogers, the same man whom Slick was giddy just to sit next to only six years earlier.

Six years. That's what it took for Slick to make the transition from goofball playing by himself to bona fide international beach volleyball player, partnered with an Olympian, a Minnesotan-turned-Californian, a lanky kid from a rural, cold-weather town to a beach bum working part-time.

"Getting that taste of two weeks in Hermosa and seeing the lifestyle out here and seeing how much better the players were, I saw the writing on the wall in that that was where the best players go," Slick said.

With the exception, of course, of the Bomgrens, who may not have the year-long training weather of California but perhaps something just as good: They have each other.

"They are super fortunate that they have each other," said Hudson Bates, the head indoor coach at Marymount University in Arlington, Va. "I would kill to have someone within even a two-hour drive from me. It would be doable to get out with each other once a week to just beat up on each other."

Bates, however, does not have that. He never has. Not in Virginia, at least. And so, four times a week, if you happen to be passing by the sand courts at Marymount, you might find a 6-foot-5, muscle-bound man donning only a weight vest and board shorts, serving balls to nobody, blocking an invisible hitter.

"It's impossible," he said, resigning himself to the fact that he will never win an AVP tournament despite making 21 main draws. "That's what makes it so frustrating. With the success that I've had the last few years, there's always a big part of me that says 'If only I could commit fully to it, what would I be able to achieve?' And that's always going to eat at me. But it's just impossible out here.

"By California standards there's a couple of single A players that live close to me and it's tough to even get those guys out to play and train. So that's why, after [2016], I figured it was about time to call it a career. That's the biggest reason."

Bates is one of dozens upon dozens of players who will be haunted by those two words: What if? As an outside hitter at George Mason, Bates finished his collegiate indoor career with 1,143 kills, third most in program history despite only playing for three years after spending his freshman year at Long Beach State. His success as a Patriot earned him an invite to train with the USA National Team in Anaheim as well as a contract to play overseas in Puerto Rico. He played three years in Puerto Rico before getting "a little burned out," and instead of re-signing with his club in Puerto Rico, he took a job running a juniors club in the U.S. One year of sitting behind a desk was enough to get him back into the game, so off he went, to Qatar, which was one part awful, one part serendipitous.

"I was happy to be over with it because it ruined something I loved," he said. "It turned it into work."

And it made him recognize his untapped love for the beach. He had played before, during summers at his parents' place in Florida, and on the side while he trained with the national team in Anaheim. But he had never fully dedicated himself to the game. When he did, in 2010, he was, by all accounts, exceptional.

At the time, the AVP was running a U-26 Tour, a developmental series that awarded the winners four automatic main draw berths on the AVP Tour. Bates, alongside partner and fellow East Coast native Mark Burik, earned those berths.

"We were super stoked about it," Bates said.

And then, in 2010, the AVP collapsed.

"We totally got screwed with that," Bates said. "And of course, when it came back they didn't honor [the main draw bids]. That really opened up my eyes. I was living in California, doing all this stuff to be a pro volleyball player, and then it folds, and it's like 'Man, this is not what I want to do with my life.'"

So he took a job back in Virginia as the director of a juniors club again, "a good wake-up call," as he says, though he couldn't fully abandon the game. Not yet. In 2014, he and Burik teamed up again, qualifying in the first two events despite living an entire country apart, and Bates would finish the season with Dave McKienzie, an indoor Olympian at the 2012 London Games, qualifying in six of seven events. By any standard, it was a successful season. But Bates couldn't shake the cost-benefit analysis.

"To go to a tournament is five days away from the family," Bates said. "And, honestly, you gotta have a partner who's understanding with that and understands that they gotta be fully on board. It's super hard for a wife to say 'Oh, go play volleyball and party afterwards and we're good.' It takes a special woman to do that. It's always tough.

"If there's any tension in our relationship it's always because of the travel. Every single time I go to a tournament it's always a week or two because I like to get out to California and train."

It wasn't the tension between Bates and his wife, Jessica, his high school sweetheart, that expedited his retirement at the age of 31, rather the sheer difficulty of competing at the level demanded in an AVP main draw while living somewhere not named California. Those long mornings by himself in Arlington, accompanied only by his weight vest and a bag of balls, had, he said, "just gotten to be too much."

This is exactly why Jon Drake believes he is so lucky. Drake lives in Milford, Ohio, a town of 6,683 that splits Clermont and Hamilton counties. There is not a natural beach within a five-hour drive, and yet, beach volleyball is one of its most popular sports, with three indoor beach facilities just a short drive from Cincinnati alone.

Those facilities are where Drake spends virtually all of his free time. When he's not working at Midwest Sports Tennis Outlet, he's playing in a league – multiple of them, five nights per week – or training at Grand Sands in neighboring Loveland.

"Not to sound like a douche," he says, laughing, "but I was, have been and, especially now, am still the hometown favorite."

When Drake was growing up, "I'll be honest, I didn't have a ton of friends," he said. He was homeschooled, took karate lessons and played basketball at the YMCA every Monday, Wednesday and Friday at the open gyms from noon to 2 in the afternoon. On the other side of the gym, the senior citizens would set up a volleyball net and slap it around, and Drake, being male and a basketball player, "thought volleyball was stupid."

Only, he didn't have much choice. Eventually, people stopped showing up to the open gyms, and Drake didn't have anybody to play hoops with. So he meandered over to the volleyball court and began hopping in games, "gorilla-slapping balls," he said. "No legal hits of any sorts."

But Drake was a competitor with an athleticism he never really tapped into. He had played in open gyms, sure, but never had the opportunity to compete in an organized sport. And on the rare occasion that a fairly talented volleyball player would walk into the YMCA, Drake would pick their brains on passing and platforms, setting and swinging. It would be wrong to say he was hooked, but he felt he might be onto something. And he was, a feeling that was validated when he was asked by a group of players if he might want to join their team in a local sand league.

"Me being homeschooled, it was really out of my comfort zone," he said. "I was 17 at the time, didn't have my license, so I'd have to find a ride. So I was like 'Let me check with my parents,' this that and the other, and they were like 'Eh, I don't know.'"

But the Drakes relented, and Jon joined his first organized – if one could call it that – competitive – if one could call it that, too – sports team.

"We were playing, I mean, straight beer, sixes, D-level volleyball," Drake said. "And I thought it was the greatest thing ever."

His ascent was a quick one. By the next season, he graduated to four-man, and the next, when he was 19, Drake began playing doubles.

"I remember a guy asking me to play, and I thought it was like Phil Dalhausser asking me to play, I was so excited and everything, and looking back on it now, this guy is like a C-level player," Drake said, laughing. "But it was huge for me at the time and from there I just started working my way through the chain. It's just been going through the local players until the point I'm at now."

The point he's at now: Partnered with a 42-year-old engineer from nearby Lebanon named Chris Luers. The partnership was forged in a manner that is typical of many successful volleyball partnerships: out of a friendly rivalry, and repeated ass-kickings.

"I saw a lot of potential in Jon before a lot of other people saw it," Luers said. "Jon is an outstanding blocker for his size. What he can do at the net is unbelievable, so when I saw that, and I saw he has a good demeanor, a good steady demeanor, not too high, not too low, it didn't take me long to realize that this guy has a future."

But at the time, Drake was the future. He was not the present. When he and Luers faced one another in local tournaments, Luers invariably came out on top, as he should have. Drake had only been playing for a handful of years. Luers had been grinding through qualifiers since 2005, before Drake had even touched a ball

It's fitting that the two would wind up playing with one another, though. Their paths to the sport are remarkably similar. Where Drake stumbled into it because there weren't enough people to play basketball, Luers was forced into it after he was deemed not good enough to play basketball, the last player cut from the University of Dayton, a perennial darling in the NCAA Tournament. Luers made his peace with being cut. He had terrible ankles, and a few more years playing basketball might have done them in for good. Maybe it was for the better, he thought. But he was an athlete, and he had a visceral need for competition that was no longer being fulfilled on the hardwood.

Good timing.

When he was cut, "that was the heyday for sand volleyball," he said. "You could turn any Sunday and watch Sinjin [Smith] and Randy [Stoklos] and Karch [Kiraly] and Kent [Steffes] playing so that kind of got in my blood."

For five years, beginning in 2000, Luers played in all the local tournaments, winning some here, placing well there, never traveling. There was an aura about the Californians. Nobody could touch them. So he didn't bother trying. But in 2005, Luers and the Ohio contingent didn't have much choice: The AVP was coming to Mason, Ohio.

"I had seen it on TV, and I didn't realize the scope of it," he said. "I hadn't realized how good these guys were."

Luers played with a fellow from Cincinnati named Jerry Dietz. Neither of them stood a hair above 6-foot-3. The thing about Jerry, though, was that he was, in demeanor, the very antithesis of Luers.

"Jerry thought we could beat anybody in the whole thing," said the endearingly, constantly understated Luers. Remarkably, they did win their first match of the qualifier, beating a pair from California in straight sets. Dietz's confidence swelled further. Luers entered a state of shock.

"I remember thinking 'We can compete out here! We can compete!'" Luers recalled. "Our next match was against Dan Mintz and Scott Hill, and they were the seven or eight seed, and I remember walking out and thinking 'We can compete against these guys.' It didn't take long to show that we were wrong. I think that was a dose of reality."

Indeed. The match was quick and decisive, 10-21, 18-21.

But hey! They had beaten a team from California!

With an extra dose of motivation, Luers took a chance: The next season, he was going to travel to California. He was going to compete against the best, on their home turf.

The 2006 season-opening tournament was in Huntington Beach. Luers and Dietz drew an 8 a.m. match against Beau Peters and Jeff Wootton, a local team, and "we just laid an egg," Luers said. "It was so discouraging. I remember walking off and saying to my buddy that 'I don't think I can ever play at this level. These guys are just too good. They train year-round, they're just too good.'"

And over the next 19 qualifiers in 12 different states with eight different partners, they were too good. Luers had chances, like a three-setter in the final qualifying round against Mike DiPierro and Steve Grotowksi at the end of 2006. Or another three-setter, two years later, in Manhattan Beach, that he and Erik Gomez lost, 16-18 in the final set in the final round. They had been up 10-5. Five points to make main draw. Five points to confirm that he was good enough.

And they blew it.

"Doubt," he admitted, "starts to creep in."

The next year, 2009, began with consecutive losses in the final qualifying round. And then, on July 1, 2009, playing alongside Danny Cook in Brooklyn, the stars and the moon aligned just right.

Chris Luers qualified for an AVP main draw.

"I'll never forget the poke over the line that I hit to win the match," he says. "It was a dream come true at that point. It's just pure euphoria. I just remember shaking everyone's hand, walking off, and I literally started to cry, and I've never cried from sports in my life."

He called his wife, who was at home with their newborn son.

"I did it!" he cried. And then she hopped in the car, put the newborn in a car seat, and booked it nine hours to Brooklyn, driving straight through the night to watch her man play in an AVP main draw the next morning.

"If anyone thinks they have the best wife ever, I challenge them to that," Luers said. "Because that's the kind of support my wife has given me."

Of course, no amount of support was going to prevent the inevitable whooping that was soon to come at the hands of Matt Olson and Kevin Wong, one of the hottest teams on Tour and the No. 3 seed for the tournament. Not that Luers cared. He didn't care that Olson and Wong put in as little effort as possible and didn't do much to hide it. He didn't care that, when he noticed their effort increase just a touch, his defense stood no chance. Olson's cannon of a swing was too powerful, far heavier and faster than anything Luers had seen in Ohio.

"I'm not going to dig these guys if they're ripping balls," Luers told Cook. Not that Cook cared, either.

They made main draw!

And after all the work, all the training, all the eating right and working out and traveling and leaving his wife and kid at home, Luers didn't win a single set in the main draw. He left Brooklyn with $240 in his pocket, earning far less than what he had spent. Didn't matter. He left with the biggest smile he'd ever had on his face.

"I couldn't have cared less about the money," he said. "Even to this day, it's never been about the money. I'm blessed to have the financial flexibility to do some things, and I don't play for the money. I just play for the love of the game. If you're writing a book about somebody who is a true qualifier – I think I'm probably about the most true qualifier there is. I'm a guy who, over the last twelve years, has played in a ton of qualifiers and usually you get the guys who jump in it, are in it for a couple years and then they move on, or you get the guys who try it and get good enough and get in the main draw, but 12 years later I'm still grinding in the qualifier. It's fun."

One by one, his partners hung it up. Cook wouldn't play in another event for four years. And in 2015, after Luers' longtime partner, Ronnie Mahlerwein, moved to Indianapolis, and Will Robbins decided to play on the NVL full-time, Luers needed a blocker.

"Chris needed somebody who basically could set a quick two-ball (a low set) out of the middle and put it there every time," Drake said. "He was basically just looking for someone who was a good setter and a decent blocker and I was basically his first candidate to play. I was pretty ecstatic and nervous because him and Ronnie had been the team to beat and I thought Chris was pretty much a wizard on the court so I very quickly jumped on it."

They played a few local tournaments and won them all, Luers banging those 2-balls out of the middle, and then they played four AVP Next tournaments, in New York, and won those, too. Before they had taken a single flight, they had qualified for the 2016 Manhattan Beach Open by winning the AVP Next regional bid in New York.

"I was thinking in my mind, we'll play Cincinnati, we'll play

Chicago, we'll take maybe one or two trips, and then I realized, he's an AVP diehard," Drake said. "He wants to do all of them."

It was enticing – and impractical. Drake gets eight or nine vacation days per year. On just the four trips to New York – eight-hour drives in which they had to leave on a Friday morning – he had burned half of them. With qualifiers taking place on Thursdays, each AVP stop for an out-of-town team demands a minimum of three days – Wednesday, Thursday, Friday – off work. The numbers didn't add up. Drake and Luers made them work anyway. They agreed that Luers would pay for the hotels and half the flights, but he'd also keep whatever meager winnings the two earned.

"I remember at those AVP Next tournaments, we'd win, and the guy would hand us the money, and I'd just take it and hand it right to Chris and say 'Ok, go book New York' or wherever it was," Drake said. "If it wasn't for Chris, I wouldn't be able to afford half the trips we made."

And he's ok with that. And therein may lie the difference between Drake and Luers and those who live in California: Volleyball is not Drake's job, nor is it his identity. Bates more or less retired because he felt like he couldn't compete at the highest level if he wasn't living in California. Drake continues to compete simply because it gives him an avenue through which to compete.

"I would get better if I were to pack up my shit and move to California, but I don't think it's a practical thing for me to just up and do," Drake said. "Then people are like 'What's your overall goal?' And I say 'To stay here and train and to make myself better.' There's a lot of guys here who are really good players. My goal is to be a competitive player who I feel like can play all the local tournaments, win all the local tournaments so I can travel to Nashville, go out to Virginia Beach when they have a big money tournament and things like that, win enough money to where I can come back after taking a day or two off work and say 'I didn't lose a penny. I went to the beach, had a great time, drank some beers on the beach and I came back and broke even.' In my mind, that's it for me. This is a hobby that I'm doing for fun and as long as I'm not losing money to support that hobby, as long as I can break even doing what I love, that's a win, more or less."

Sometimes they do more than break even. Four months prior to the 2016 AVP New Orleans Open, Drake and Luers had played in an indoor sand series in Nashville, winning the finals and the $3,000 in cash that came with it.

"Still to this day all of my coworkers give me crap about playing volleyball, saying 'Oh, you're gonna go train with all the girls today?'" Drake said. "They'll give me crap, but after I came back from that tournament in Nashville, me and Luers won three thousand bucks, we came home and I went to work Monday morning, and I showed them that and they were kinda like 'Ok, whatever.' They thought we were just out there playing and drinking beers and dancing on the court kind of thing."

Was it AVP? Maybe not. But it was still a beach volleyball trip that earned the two a couple grand and an office's worth of respect.

The only thing left, then, was the respect of the AVP Tour. Which is, of course, much more difficult to earn than from a few cubicle mates and coffee buddies.

Chris Luers is, like anybody in the sport of beach volleyball, a Karch Kiraly enthusiast. How could he not be? The guy won 148 tournaments, three Olympic gold medals, the most dominant player of all-time. A quirky habit of Kiraly's, however, is that he never checked to see whom he played beforehand. He'd simply get to the beach, warm up, and whomever showed up on the court was who he played. By Kiraly's thinking, if he played his game, it didn't much matter who he played. He was going to win.

Throughout the 2016 season, Luers gave the Kiraly anti-preparation theory a spin. And when he made his way to his court at the Huntington Beach Open on May 4, 2016, he damn near fell over. There was one team – one team! – in the entire draw that Drake and Luers absolutely knew they didn't want to draw: Orlando Irizarry and Roberto Rodriguez-Bertran, the Puerto Rican national team.

"Who is that team we didn't want?" Drake asked when the draw was released, and he saw their names next to Irizarry and Rodriguez-Bertran, known as "Rafu" amongst his beach volleyball peers.

"Irizarry and Rafu," Luers replied.

Drake's heart sunk.

"Really?" he thought. "We're gonna come all the way out here and our first freakin' match of the day – I mean, Chris literally stated, 'That's the one team I didn't want to draw first.'"

Luers, hilariously, had no idea until he stepped onto the court and saw the Puerto Ricans.

"Ok," he said to himself, "this is how it's gonna be."

But then the damndest thing happened: Drake and Luers smashed them in the first set and rallied after dropping the second, winning the match 21-15, 18-21, 15-12.

"As soon as we won that match I thought we were in the main draw," Drake said. "I checked my phone and I had like a billion texts and I was just so, so excited, especially to see how excited Chris was."

Problem was, they had three more matches to win, and not enough gas in the tank to win them, losing two rounds later to Adam Cabbage and John Moran, a pair who were main draw regulars. A tough loss, but the trip was viewed as a success: They proved they could hang. They beat one of the best teams in the whole tournament. The AVP's stop in Seattle was just a month away.

Since the tournament wouldn't be in California, the field wouldn't be as strong. That's how the thinking went, at least. That would be their time. Until it wasn't. They lost in the first round, to a team they thought they should have beat. A $500 flight for one hour-long match.

"It definitely was a little slap to the face," Drake said. "It definitely sucked going all the way up there because we both love that location."

Luers wondered if they should call it quits, if this was something they were willing to do. Drake was. He still had some money in the budget. So they went back to work, concentrating on finding each other's sets better. Drake worked on peeling off the net faster. It worked. Kind of. Two weeks later, in New York, they won their first two qualifying matches, making it to the final round. And lost again.

They skipped the next tournament, a week later in San Francisco. Then came Manhattan Beach, their first main draw, automatically in because the four AVP Next tournaments they won.

"It's just so much bigger, there's so many more people there, it's just such a cool atmosphere," Drake said of main draw. "Having those nerves on Wednesday, getting touches in. We don't have to worry about waking up the next morning, 42 points and it might be over. We can have some drinks, walk around, cheer on our friends, watch some really good matches, just thinking 'Geez it would really suck to be playing right now, because it's a ridiculous qualifier.' It's a much easier, relaxing trip. We knew we weren't leaving on Thursday night after a qualifier. It was nice having that safety harness, knowing that if we have a bad game, we have a second chance."

They lost their first match, to the Bomgrens, and then the second as well. Their trip over in two matches. But Drake had finally had his taste of main draw, his taste of success in beach volleyball. And there was but one more tournament left to have it again: Chicago. And when Luers' poke shot dropped in the third and final qualifying round, he had it again, his first main draw via qualifier, an indelible feeling.

"It was the happiest I've seen Luers, to finally earn our way in," Drake said. "That was for sure the best feeling I've ever had, of any match I've ever had. That win was really, really awesome."

Of the 24 teams in the main draw, just four were made up of players

191

living outside of California, all of whom were knocked out in three matches or less.

And yet, "if I had to do it again," Luers said, "I wouldn't trade it for the world."

AFTERWORD

The Wonderful Misery of Chasing Dreams

t was September of 2018, and I stood behind the press box, watching two volleyball matches, watching nothing.

My AVP season – my first real season as a beach volleyball player, as I see it – had ended. I was lost in thought, thinking about Chicago, thinking about Austin, site of my first main draw, thinking about how blink-and-you-missed it fast the year had gone by, thinking about how slowly it had sometimes seemed to drag on.

A tap on my shoulder. A photographer. I like photographers. They make for fun conversations, because to be a photographer – a good one, an exceptional one – means you are obsessed with your craft and funny things like light, angles, how elements of nature play off of one another to create the perfect moment to capture.

The photographer extended his hand, said it was fun to shoot me this season, and even more fun to follow along. He mentioned what a great season I had. I looked down. I didn't know. It had ended on a sour note, the most recent one a 21-19, 21-12 pounding in the final round of the Chicago qualifier, less than 24 hours before, was still an open wound.

And then he said something quite profound, not only in its depth but also in its simplicity.

"You're going for your dreams," he said, and I'll pause there to tell you this: I hear this lots, multiple times per day on some occasions. Many tell me how jealous they are that I'm out in California, living the dream life, chasing this, getting after that, and how great it would be to do what I am so very blessed to do. I paused there because he then added an addendum that few ever care to consider: "That's awesome, because I think one of the most difficult things to do is go for your dreams."

I loved that. Because it's true. Billy Allen wrote an excellent blog post after the Hermosa Beach Open, where he and Ryan Doherty took a tough loss in the finals after leading 14-12 in the third set. He mentioned something a buddy said, how most office workers can't empathize with the emotional low Billy was currently experiencing, but they'd probably, strangely, love to be able to feel an emotion so deeply.

Chasing dreams at once offers the highest of the highs and the lowest of the lows. It's a bit like being in love, really, and here I'll call to mind a scene from the movie Hitch, where Will Smith, attempting to win back Eva Mendes, yells at her that he "just wants to feel miserable! Like, really miserable, because, hey, if that what it takes for me to be happy – well that didn't come out right."

It kind of did come out right, though, because only love can make a man feel so miserable, and yet to feel that miserable means you might just be in love – with a person, a craft, something – a sensation to which there is no comparison.

I don't particularly enjoy being miserable after losses, but frankly, I'd be a bit concerned if I weren't miserable after a loss, if I were simply ok with it. That would mean that, somewhere along the lines, I had stopped caring, and if I had stopped caring, then was I really chasing my dreams at all?

So I smiled at the photographer. I suppose, when compared to the last year and the one before that, it had been a great season, one filled with highs, one filled with lows, one laced with euphoria, one replete with feelings on the other side of the spectrum.

It had been what chasing dreams seems to be all about.

And here's the thing I learned about chasing dreams: Throughout the process of pursuing one goal, that big one you think you want to achieve so badly and that when you get there everything will simply fall into place, you incidentally accrue experiences and memories and stories and moments that, in retrospect, so heavily outweigh the feeling of accomplishment you get when attaining the original goal.

Just the other night, my girlfriend Delaney Knudsen and I were discussing our favorite stops of the year. Most would assume mine would be Austin, site of my first main draw, site of that big goal at the end of the tunnel that I thought would be the fountain of all eternal happiness.

I surprised myself with my own answer.

Austin was my least favorite, and ranking far ahead of those were – shockingly – New York, San Francisco, Seattle, and now Chicago.

Hermosa, where I made my second main draw and my first Saturday, and Austin were where my volleyball goals had been realized, and they're nowhere near the top of my favorite weekends of the season.

The other four now hold experiences I'll cherish for as long as my memory serves me well enough to recall them. It was in New York that I took a ferry – a ferry! – to a beach volleyball tournament, passing by Lady Liberty on my way there, with a fellow freelance journalist, Maria Marino, with whom I traded breakfast and freelancing stories and tidbits.

In a few years, I'll forget the score of my match, a disappointing finish, to be sure. But I will not forget sailing past the Statue of Liberty to get to a beach volleyball tournament. Nor will I forget my parents coming in town, making the drive north from Maryland, to see their first AVP, introducing them to all of my incredibly accomplished friends. My dad, who has been to countless sporting events of all types, said it was one of his favorites of all time.

I'd agree, even though my weekend was cut short, my worst finish of the year. I agree because the goodness of people shined as bright as it ever will, as men and women like Reid Priddy and Jeremy Casebeer, Casey Patterson and Phil Dalhausser, Sara Hughes and Eric Zaun treated my parents like their own.

I went home the next day, feasted on crabs, drank too much beer with my brothers, knocked out on my couch.

The sport that has taken me 3,000 miles from my family is the same that brought me right back to it.

Two weeks later we were in San Francisco. After another early loss, Tri Bourne and I stole away to Bear Valley, kidnapping Delaney, to see his sister's family. And it was in Bear Valley that I fell in love with Tri's family and probably began to feel pangs of something similar with the one we kidnapped.

What's a main draw compared to that?

It almost seems silly to think that making main draw had been the goal, and not the experiences that will be etched into memory far longer.

Those experiences are the fuel that keeps the pursuing of those goals possible. You might be able to put a destination – making a main draw, making a Saturday, making a Sunday – into a GPS, but you still need the fuel to get there. Without those, simply making main draw won't be enough. It never would.

Perhaps Austin is my least favorite stop because it tore down the mythology of making a main draw. I had built it up in my mind. Everything will be different, I thought. But it wasn't. Hanging in the player's tent was no different than hanging at Tri's house. It was just hotter, the couches weren't as comfy, and we didn't drink as much wine. Playing against Billy and Ryan in my first main draw match was no different than practicing in Hermosa Beach. There were just a couple extra people there to watch, and a little more money on the line.

It was, simply put, still volleyball.

There's more to life than volleyball.

This is not to say goals are useless, or materialistic, or any other crap you'll hear unmotivated and lazy people say about lofty goals. This is not to say that I don't go into tournaments wanting nothing more than to make a main draw, and then push it further from there.

Goals, ambition, aspirations – they're all vital to a life of value, or at least they are to mine. For without those goals, without that burning desire to make those main draws, I don't go to Austin, and New York, and Seattle, and San Francisco. I don't look at a breathtaking galaxy of stars in Bear Valley, California, deep into the night, feeling a sense of contentment and stillness that's difficult to imagine unless you've taken the time to do it.

I don't reconnect with old friends or make so many new ones I've come to admire and respect and love. I don't go deep down the surfing YouTube rabbit hole with Spencer McLaughlin and Tri, laughing well into an Oakland night. I don't drown in deep dish pizza with my boy from the south, Matt Blanke, and get caught in a Windy City thunderstorm on a pier with Delaney, both of us too stoked to see a thunderstorm to care one bit about getting wet and cold and probably sick. I don't see the Statue of Liberty, or go home. I don't launch a podcast, give players a much-needed platform.

Without those goals, those experiences I've mentioned don't become experiences at all.

Without those goals, there would be no dream to chase. And without that chase would be a life devoid of my fondest memories, memories that will last far longer than a couple thousand bucks in prize money and the forever enigmatic title of professional athlete.

We may not get rich playing beach volleyball. Hell, we might even lose money doing so. I'm ok with that. For what I've gained, and likely what every other player has as well, is worth far more than a paycheck or two of prize money.

A new goal-setting process begins.

There are more GPS coordinates to put into the map.

Between those coordinates are what life, for me, for most beach volleyball players, is all about.

Adventures await.

ACKNOWLEDGEMENTS

I've made my best attempt to minimize the amount of debt I go into in life. With this book, however, I became deeply indebted to so many people I cannot even begin to count, though I do know, with absolute and unequivocal certainty, where to start: the players.

I interviewed more than 100 players for this book, which is actually split into two – the second will hopefully be finished in a year or two – and for that, I am forever in your debt. All of you. You lent me the two most precious things in life: your time and your stories. These are things you cannot get back. More than that, you trusted me with both of them, and for that, no amount of thank yous will ever be enough. This small bit in the back of the book you contributed greatly to is, simply, the best I can do.

An extra massive thank you must go to Tri Bourne, who wrote the phenomenal forward for this book and was the very first interview for it. I remember it as if it were yesterday: I was sitting on my bed in my studio in Newport Beach. We spoke for nearly two hours, and when I hung up, I just stared at the phone.

Did I just talk to Tri Bourne for two hours? Tri Bourne! Two hours!

This was going to be the greatest, most fun project I could possibly work on.

I wasn't wrong.

Over the next two years, Tri has become much more than the guy who wrote the forward and delivered a wonderful interview. He's become a podcast partner, a coach, an incredible friend and, most importantly and irreplaceably, a big brother to me in California. I cannot wait to see what the future brings for Tri.

A thanks, as well, to Ann Maynard, the editing wizard who encouraged me to split the book into two, which only, as obvious as it was, occurred to me after she recommended it. She opened my eyes to the many, many flaws in this book. Hopefully I fixed them well enough to be passable to you, the reader.

And, of course, a thank you to my incredible friends from home (Hampstead, Maryland), most of whom do not know beach volleyball from cricket, a side out from a shoot set. And yet y'all are the first ones to wish me luck, to say congratulations, even when you don't know what it is you're wishing me luck for, or why, exactly, you're congratulating me. From kindergarten to nearly age 30, y'all have been the support system that no other group of friends can replicate. I love every single one of you beyond words.

To my parents and brothers, who will never issue the words: "You can't." It's been the constant drumbeat of my life: *You can, you can, you can.* It doesn't matter what – golf, basketball, writing, podcasting, this weird beach volleyball thing I picked up on a whim and moved across the country to pursue. Your belief in me has been as important as any tangible skill you have impressed upon me, and those are innumerably many.

And, alas, to the beach volleyball community, which has supported and inspired me like no other community I've been a part of, and in particular, the greatest human I know, Delaney Knudsen. I cannot describe how much it means to roll out to the beach and have individuals introduce themselves just to tell me they appreciate my writing, or the podcast, or how open I am with my failures and successes – what few there are in that department – as a player. When I began writing about this sport, I did so for free, and for fun. Your feedback and immovable support has made living this life a reality, and I am forever indebted to you for that.

It is the very backbone of this book.

See you all on the beach.

CPSIA information can be obtained
at www.ICGtesting.com
Printed in the USA
FSHW011301250620
71553FS